In All Your Ways

Dr. Ron Long

IN ALL YOUR WAYS

Dr. Ron Long

Copyright
1985

UPLIFT MINISTRIES
3663 Finger Creek Drive
Lilburn, Georgia 30247

Brentwood Christian Press
Columbus, GA 31906

ISBN 0-916573-50-8

Foreword

Ron Long is a "bottom-line" type fellow who speaks directly and to the point. In our day when time must be seized and utilized for the maximum good such style is even more in demand.

He combines tasteful satire, down-home reporting, and humor to make the experience of being confronted with the truth a memorable as well as enjoyable one.

To be read at a sitting or in snatches of time as they are made available will be equally edifying and enjoyable. Areas not often dealt with in one volume are delved into with zeal and clarity making this volume a veritable handbook on life's episodes.

I commend to you both the author and the volume with excitement and anticipation.

-Dr. Jack Taylor, President
Dimensions in Christian Living
Fort Worth, Texas

Dedication

To my family -- my wife Lethia, and our three children, Stan, Chris, and Kelly, who have made all the difference in all my ways.

To my church family -- the extraordinary people of Glenwood Hills Baptist Church, who join with me in pointing others toward The Way.

Acknowledgements

My Special thanks to Sandra Johnson, who encouraged me to begin, refused to let me quit, and then ordered me to finish. Her inspiration, ability, and energy made this work possible.

Introduction

"Two roads diverged in a yellow wood, and sorry I could not be one traveler and travel both, long I stood . . ." No respectable education could be complete without the hallowed words of Robert Frost indelibly inscribed in the memory. The poem is indeed a classic, both in form and structure and in the message it conveys. But for those of us who are less scholarly minded, the work holds another fascination. From our current fast-paced view, it seems so nostalgic and almost eutopic to be pulled in only two directions at one time.

The one phrase used again and again to describe our society is that we are growing more and more fragmented. Society in general is not my specialty. People are my specialty, and as individuals we so easily become classic examples of Mr. Webster's explanation of the term:

Fragment --
 1. part broken off or undetached
 2. portion unfinished or incomplete
 3. odd piece, bit, or scrap

Our lives consist of many roles, many functions, and many areas demanding so much of our time, energies, and devotion, that we come to exist as many fragments or tiny pieces, rather than the whole and complete personality that the Lord intends for us to be. Even as Christians, we often place our love and service for Him in certain areas of our day, while excluding the Saviour from others.

The purpose of this book is to help you begin to realize the reality of Christ in everything you do. So many times, we see Him only in the tall white columns, crossed steeple, or stained glass windows, when the true difference He wants to make in us exists among the day-to-day grind. Whether dealing with your family, struggling to succeed in business, enjoying leisure, or experiencing difficulty, Christ is the central factor centrifuging all that you are into all that He wants you to be. While going in many ways, you are truly moving in only one direction -- closer to the foot of the Cross.

> *"Trust in the Lord with all your heart; and lean not unto your own understanding. In all your ways acknowledge Him, and He shall direct your paths."*
>   Proverbs 3:5 and 6

Uplift Ministries

Dr. Ron Long, through the organization of Uplift Ministries, has a growing tape ministry. With both single tapes consisting of two messages, and sets of various sermon series, Dr. Long offers the best in expository preaching. His Biblical knowledge and practical application encourage the listener to realize that knowing the Lord is the vital thread interwoven through all that we are and all that we do. The following tapes are currently available:

Singles
  I. S.B.C. Pastor's Conference (Side 1)
     Criswell Bible Institute (Side 2)
  II. Requirements and Results of Revival (Side 1)
      Lordship of Christ (Side 2)
  III. God's Blueprint for Family Living (Side 1)
       Reality of the Rapture (Side 2)

Sets
  I. God's Pattern for Family Living (Set of 4)
  II. Jesus in the Tabernacle (Set of 6)
  III. Spiritual Warfare: Putting on the Armor (Set of 4)

For further information on these and other available titles, contact:

UPLIFT MINISTRIES
3663 Finger Creek Drive
Lilburn, Georgia 30247

1
The Way of Feelings

IN THIS CHAPTER . . . .

"The Giant Oak Tree That Fell"
Put Away Childish Things
The Breaking Point
Bad Words Are Never Good Words
Don't Be A Postmortem Person
Carrying Out The Garbage In Your Life
Many Try To Live On 'Fantasy Island'
Searching For The Fountain Of Youth
Spare Parts For Christians
About Finding The "Scapegoats"
Putting Away Childish Things
How To Be A Successful Worrier
A New Creature
Your Attitude Will Determine How Old You Are
Alone But Not Lonely
"The Burnout Syndrome"
The Cutting Edge
"Make Peace And Retain Inner Calm"
Be Content With Your Life
Balloons Or Blessings?
Don't Let Past Mistakes Bind You

"THE GIANT OAK TREE THAT FELL"

As a small boy growing up, my heart was attached to the big oak tree behind our home. I loved that old oak tree.

In the summer its massive branches would burst forth with life, and the green leaves would begin to cover the bare limbs with its spring fashion. In the fall of the year the colors changed to the beautiful browns and golds of autumn. Over the years I've seen the limbs of that giant oak tree as they swayed with the winds of March. I've also seen them drooped with the ice of January.

This oak tree was a favorite place of mine. It was in this oak tree that I carved my sweetheart's initials, and it was in this tree that the favorite swing was hung. Then one day I noticed that though it was spring, this great tree was not clothed in beautiful green leaves as it had been in earlier years. Soon the leaves that were on it turned to a dark brown prematurely.

What the winds of March could not do and what the ice of winter could not do, an insect was now accomplishing. A small beetle had entered into that giant tree. That beetle had brought his hordes of little friends along with him. Although that insect was so small that a man could crush it between his thumb and forefinger, it could, with the help of all its companions, fell the giant oak tree.

There are those in life who can withstand the giant temptations. They will not bend, nor will they break. They will not succumb to the big, so-called sins, but they yield time and time again to the "little beetle" sins. Wrong attitudes, resentments, anger, worry, fear, hostility and an unforgiving temper are nothing but little beetles that will rob us of the blessings and will fell the giant oak tree.

PUT AWAY CHILDISH THINGS

When the hectic pace of phones ringing, typewriters clicking, a mound of mail and five people calling, "Pastor" get to be a little more than I can sort out, I love to slide out the side door of the church office and go around to the other side of the building. Then I find a different kind of scurrying, for the classes of our Pre-School and Kingergarten are in full swing each morning.

I love to watch these three and four and five year olds as they go about their learning processes. They try and try, and if success doesn't come quickly, the lower lip is the first to react, for it begins to display itself in a rolled out fashion that could catch rain should a shower occur. Sharing toys and taking turns are not natural instincts at this age. Fights, screams, and tears are immediate reactions until the children learn that they cannot always have their own way about everything. With a chuckle, I enjoy watching their antics, knowing most of the problems they experience at this time will be outgrown in the months and years ahead.

The Apostle Paul reminded us that we pass from childhood actions when we become adults, and our understanding changes. He says we must put away childish things. Yet we all know some areas of our lives where we are still thinking and behaving as children.

What have you failed to put away? Perhaps it is a grudge over some incident where you feel you were wronged. Maybe fears of any of a hundred varieties keep you from living life fully. Worry cripples you and drains energies that could be much better used. Jealousy, that green-eyed monster, shifts from toy ownership to much more destructive things such as positions, prestige, or possessions.

As the teachers guide our children, the Lord will guide you to rid your life of these destructive, childish things. A three year old is vastly different in May than he was on that first day of kindergarten in September, but it occurs over days and months of careful effort and instruction. You can become a vastly different, happier, and more productive person as you allow the Saviour to grow you.

THE BREAKING POINT

I love the Ordinance of Baptist. I love all the significance it holds in terms of submission and service. I love the feel of the water and those who enter the baptismal. There is a meaningful feeling to step into that pool each Sunday morning. However, last week there was another kind of pool at our church which created quite a different feeling and reaction; for, you see, our nursery wing was flooded under several inches of water, following the freezing and thawing of pipes in the walls. The words, "What must we do!" were resounding throughout the halls.

Such a happening is an inevitability each winter as the temperature plummets with no one aware and the water becomes frozen overnight in the pipes. As it solidifies, the expanding volume of the ice breaks the lines at one or several spots. Let the thermometer begin to rise and the damage caused by the pressure within becomes all too evident.

Pressure has become an accepted part of our daily lives. To a certain degree, it can be helpful in that it makes us move forward and accomplish many good things. It makes us conscientious and leaves little room for laziness. Too often our healthy desire to be a good person and do well leads us to feel the push and pull of a thousand different things. Little by little the pressure builds and the damage it does will begin to be evidenced in many ways. Like the out-of-sight pipes in the walls, we may not be aware of the problem within ourselves while the stress overshadows more and more of our daily lives, dampens our joy and drowns the spark of uniqueness we each possess.

As Christians we are not closed away somewhere, a victim of whatever life may send us. We would think it ridiculous to picture Christ wringing His hands over some circumstance with a knot behind his shoulders. Therefore, if He is with us and in us, it is just as ridiculous for us to be in that position. When we begin to forget this fact and build up like a pressure cooker, it is time to go back to the first pool -- the baptistry -- back to the time when we first believed. The certainty and assurance we feel at that point is ours to claim each day. When we do all that is within ourselves to get to that point, then we know the victory is ours to claim.

BAD WORDS ARE NEVER GOOD WORDS

Whenever I reach the point of saying, "Well, nothing can top that," something always does! I thought I had heard them all until I read in *Time Magazine* of that which is taking place in Zurich, Switzerland.

In this city, an obscenity hotline was installed. Subscribers to this service receive a code name and a secret telephone number. At any hour of the day or night, for about $1 a minute, they can talk to four men and four women who will cheerfully and willingly listen to all of their obscenities.

This service reflects the changing nature of profanity. Movies and television now allow "street language" to come into our dens and living rooms. It has even been pointed out that many professional men, successful men, have been users of profanity. Men in history like our first President George Washington, all the way to the present Dodger Manager Tommy Lasorda, have used profanity. As a matter of fact, Lasorda used 144 obscenities in a brief pep talk to his Dodger team.

Psychologist Chaytor Mason, in commenting on the wide use of profanity made the statement that he thinks that it is a healthy emotional outlet.

Somewhere along the way we have forgotten or simply ignored the fact that God said "not." God never says "not" unless there's a reason, and the reason is always for our own advantage. It is for our own good that God says not to take His name in vain.

When one senselessly and uselessly decides to do that, it is not a reflection upon God, it is simply a reflection upon the individual. It indicates to the listener that here is an individual who is not in control of his emotions to the extent that he can speak in a way that is offensive both to the listener and to God.

"Thou shalt not take the name of the Lord thy God in vain." Exodus 20:7.

† † †

DON'T BE A POSTMORTEM PERSON

A few years ago we had a bush in our yard that we called a "snowball bush." It had big, beautiful, snow white flowers on it that looked like spring-time snowballs. Once in a while, though, we would see a snowball bush whose flowers were tainted with a slight trace of pink or blue. They were still snowball bushes, but they were slightly off-colored.

What had happened to those bushes was that a chemical had found its way into the soil around them. As it seeped down into the earth, it worked its way into the root system of the plant. While the bush still lived, the once pure, beautiful white blooms had become off-colored.

There are people whose lives become off-colored, like the snowball bush. I often think of these people as postmortem people. What is a postmortem person, you ask? Well, it's someone who is constantly digging up the past, living and reliving all of the heartbreak and disappointment of yesterday's mistakes and failures.

The postmortem person becomes so overpowered with a lifetime's worth of tragedy and failure that he begins to feel that his life has no value. He begins to ask questions like, "Why was I ever born?" His accomplishments become meaningless, so that, after 25 years on the job, he finds himself asking, "Why am I doing this job?"

No one has to live constantly doing a postmortem on the past. There is a way to properly deal with it. We must recognize our failures and admit our mistakes. But then, rather than allow our yesterdays to off-color our todays with defeat, we can claim our Lord's forgiveness. Having done that, we need to recognize that He has forgiven us. The Lord said, *"Though your sins be as scarlet, they shall be white as snow"* (Isaiah 1:18). When we have asked for the Lord's forgiveness, our sins aren't covered up, simply to be dug up and relived again and again. They have been washed away, cleansed. We can be as a pure snowball bush, as white as ever.

CARRYING OUT THE GARBAGE IN YOUR LIFE

For some reason, it has always been my job to carry out the garbage. Over the years I've watched as we've gone through the "garbage transition." We began with the simple brown bag from the grocery store, and then moved on to the plastic bag. Now, that wasn't enough. Next we moved on to the plastic bags that have straps that you can tie together to close the bag before you take it out of the garbage can. But wait! We've progressed even further than that! We are now able to use deodorized garbage bags! Regardless of how far we've come, though, one thing still remains the same. I'm still the one who has to take out the garbage.

Well, you may have guessed that carrying the garbage out is not one of my favorite pastimes. I just can't bring myself to jump up and down with glee, shouting, "It's time to carry out the garbage!" It's just the opposite. This is what happens: "The garbage bag is full." No response. Next directive: "The garbage needs to be emptied." Still no response. Finally, the third mandate: "If you don't carry out the garbage, I will." Now, that does it. You see, I know she won't carry out the garbage -- but I'd better! So I get up, and out it goes. I always have to carry out the garbage.

There's a lesson to be learned from emptying the garbage. It's not something that I alone have to do. Everyone needs to learn how to "dump the garbage" in their lives. I don't mean the stuff you carry out in the "Glad bags." The kind of garbage we have to learn to get rid of is mental garbage. It's the negative thoughts and ideas that people store in their minds and hearts until they become real "stinkers." If we don't learn to clear our minds of this kind of garbage, it can develop into serious maladjustments.

Instead of storing the garbage, we need to learn to store positive thoughts. To do that, we must learn to fill our minds continually with positive things. Learn to count your blessings, taking time to name them, one by one. When you spend time thinking of all of the positive things God has done in your life, you'll find that these are the things that are stored in your mind.

At the close of each day, let your last thoughts be spent in thanking God for the blessings of that day. When you do this, you'll wake up in the morning with the mindset that says, *"This is the day which the Lord hath made; we will rejoice and be glad in it"* (Psalm 118:14). And by the way, when you begin to store up these kind of thoughts, you'll never have to "dump the garbage."

† † †

MANY TRY TO LIVE ON 'FANTASY ISLAND'

Many people are content to live their lives pursuing their own version of "Fantasy Island." In their minds, Ricardo Montalban is just around the next corner, always dressed in a white tuxedo, with Tattoo by his side, and ever ready to fulfill any fantasy they desire. In this fantasy world they are completely separated from all the problems and displeasure, and are surrounded by beauty. In their minds they would be content to live out their lives here, never coming into contact with the realm of reality.

But "Fantasy Island" is just a fantasy. It's not reality, and cannot be viewed as reality. It is the denial of truth. Truth is frequently looked upon as being perplexing, and painful, yet the Bible teaches that *". . . ye shall know the truth, and the truth shall make you free"* (John 8:32).

The truth as to who we are and where we are going in life will free us from living out our lives in a world of fantasy. When we live in the reality of our world, we are free to be and do all that God intends for us to be and do. Only then can we make a difference in the world in which we live.

"Fantasy Island" does not exist. It is not real. Ricardo Montalban and Tattoo aren't ever going to meet us at the airport. We are going to live day by day in the reality of this world.

The only way that life can be lived fully, successfully, and in reality, is to be freed to be the person that God desires for us to be; to do that which God desires for us to do. *"Ye shall know the truth, and the truth shall make you free . . ."* This truth frees you to live in reality.

SEARCHING FOR THE FOUNTAIN OF LOVE

Ponce de Leon spent his life searching for the Fountain of Youth. He believed there was such a fountain, and that if he could find it, and drink from it, he would remain forever youthful.

A lot of people today spend their lives looking . . . searching. They're searching for the same fountain Ponce de Leon searched for, but they've camouflaged it. They don't call it a Fountain of Youth any more, they call it love. They spend all of their time and energy looking for love, believing that if they find it, it will stir some chords within them that will transform them from 45 to 18.

So, they keep looking. Some people have drawn the conclusion that they'll find it just off Madison Avenue, or down the street from Yale University. Others are certain that they'll find a book in the local bookstore that will tell them how and where to find their "fountain." We keep talking about romance, about needing it, and wanting it. We watch "Love Boat" and wonder why it never floated by us, or we see "Dallas" and not understand why we aren't living on that beautiful ranch in Texas. We watch "Fantasy Island" and create for an hour our own fantasy, but when the hour is over the fantasies elude us.

I guess the reason we keep looking for love without ever finding it is that we look in the wrong places. We'll never have an understanding of love, or of the expressing of love, until we realize that love is inward. It's the kind of love that doesn't ask for anything in return. It's Biblical love.

There are two aspects of Biblical love. First, Biblical love is unconditional. It says I love you regardless. And, second, Biblical love is unreciprocal. It says I love you, and I don't need anything in return. This kind of love is inward. It's the kind of love that was expressed in its most meaningful sense when He communicated love in who He was. The Fountain of Love flows from the one who understood and communicated love. His name is Jesus.

† † †

SPARE PARTS FOR CHRISTIANS?

Like the myriad number of fast-food places that line the highways, a little less frequently but just as varied, automobile parts shops pop up: Parts Country; American Auto Parts; #1 Parts, Inc.; Giant Discount Auto Parts; Super-A; NAPA; Tiger; U-Name-It-We-Got-It.

Just think, wouldn't it be great if there were a spare parts shop for Christians? Imagine picking up a shiny new resolve to serve the Lord. Or, how about a pert new witness for only $19.95?

You could even buy a prayer life still in the box for only $69.95 (assembly required). The deluxe prayer life would be available for $20 extra. Perhaps you would be interested in a new Spirit with chrome side pipes for $114.95, installed. (West Coast prices slightly higher.)

Well, of course, there are no such spare parts shops for Christians. However, we can sure have the old parts "rebuilt." God gives us a promise in Isaiah 40:31 that *"they that wait upon the Lord shall renew their strength; they shall mount up with wings as eagles; they shall run, and not be weary; and they shall walk, and not faint."*

Are you discouraged? Are you tired and weak? If you are, then go to God and be renewed! His work carries an eternal guarantee!

† † †

ABOUT FINDING THE "SCAPEGOATS"

I am sure that you have heard of that phrase, "Well, he was made the scapegoat." It is said most often when we do something wrong or we fail to do something that we know we should have done. We look for a "scapegoat."

Most people feel that they must find someone or something to blame. We seek to evade our own personal responsibility for mistakes and misdeeds by blaming circumstances or other people. This is called "finding the scapegoat."

As we continue to be informed about the labor and management entanglements of the automobile industry, we see that each one blames the other. It seems that neither wants to acknowledge responsibility for the problem. Each keeps looking for the scapegoat.

A carpenter goes out and begins his daily work. When he misses the nail and hits his own thumb, he cries out and, either does, or is tempted to, curse the hammer. The hammer becomes the scapegoat.

How many golfers have stood looking down at that little white ball with a putter in his hand, knowing that he needs to make this putt, for it will determine if he wins the match or loses. He "lines up the putt" and taps the ball, only to watch it roll very gently by the "lip" of the cup. When he stands up straight, he looks at the end of the putter and comments, "I need a new putter." The putter becomes the scapegoat.

You smelled the unpleasant odor when you walked into the house. You did not need a word of explanation from your wife informing you that she had burned the roast. When you inquired about what had happened, she was quick to inform you that it was the new electric range. The "new electric range" became the scapegoat.

If we are so intent in using this Biblical term, we need to find out where the term comes from and what it means. The Israelites had an annual "Day of Attonement." The ritual of the scapegoat was part of the Day of Atonement observance.

On that day the high priest confessed his sins before the Lord. Then the high priest took two goats and sacrificed one as a sin offering to God. He placed his hands on the head of the second goat and confessed the sins of Israel. Then this "scapegoat" was driven out into the wilderness -- never to be seen again. It is from this ancient ritual that we get the term "scapegoat."

We cannot really continue to deal with our problems and failures by finding scapegoats. The prodigal son is a clear illustration of how we must deal with our problems and not search for scapegoats. When the prodigal son returned to his father (Luke

15:11-24), he did not blame his father's restrictions or the economic conditions of the country where he traveled for his troubles. It was only when he "came to himself" that he had the courage to return home to the love of his father.

Our Christian experience gives us strength in finding forgiveness rather than scapegoats for reality. True Christian repentance is simply abandoning scapegoats and experiencing the father's forgiveness.

† † †

PUTTING AWAY CHILDISH THINGS

During a ceremony held in Mexico City on May 2, 1977, about 120 children were injured when clusters of hydrogen-filled balloons burst into flames. The police report stated that some of the children were severely burned as a result of the accident. Other children were trampled in the panic to escape the flames. What had appeared to be a simple and childish balloon-fest had resulted in a terrible tragedy.

Christians today are being offered many bright and attractive "experiences" which, when compared to traditional Christianity, seem very desirable and colorful. These many different "experiences" often appear to be delightfully entertaining.

Unfortunately, however, some believers have been harmed through these experiences when, after a while, they have burst and involved people in emotional damage.

The Apostle Paul affirmed that when he became a man, he put away childish things. *"When I was a child I spake as a child, I understood as a child, I thought as a child; but when I became a man, I put away childish things"* (I Corinthians 13:11).

Let us follow his example and not be content to be caught up in immature emotional experiences. Instead, we should let our experience in Christ be a growing and maturing process.

† † †

HOW TO BE A SUCCESSFUL WORRIER:

LET GOD HELP OUT

There are probably many areas in your life that you would like to be successful in, but I'm quite sure that worrying isn't one of them! With all of the things we would like to accomplish, it's absolutely amazing how much time and practice we dedicate to worrying! With many people it's a daily routine.

Worry has been compared to rocking in a rocking chair -- you put forth a lot of work, but you never get anywhere! With the complex lives that most people seem to lead today, worries can begin to multiply until it seems that there's no way out. Many people try to escape into some sort of fantasy land where there are no problems, nothing to worry about, often through the use of alcohol or drugs. When that attempt fails, many will try other avenues of human effort. Finally, in desperation, they cry out to God. But, at least they finally do cry out to Him.

The most important step in dealing with worries is to let God in on them. You are important to Him, and He wants you to share your worries with Him. In I Peter 5:7, the Bible encourages us by saying, *"Casting all your anxiety upon Him because He cares for you."* This is a tremendously comforting thought. God really cares for us . . . for me individually.

We learn from the Bible that the way to be a "successful worrier" is to let God in on our worries so He can help. And when the matter rests in God's care, there is no longer any reason for us to continue worrying. When we realize that God will guide us through all of life's situations, we may even reach the point where we can express ourselves by saying, "What? Me worry?"

† † †

A NEW CREATURE

Nepal is a country of fifteen million people bordering China. There is a street in Nepal named Freak Street. Freak Street got its name from the thousands of long haired wanderers who flocked in during the 60's and 70's. The thing that caught my attention about this little country in the Himalayas was a story about a boy who spends all his days on Freak Street. This boy is a heroin addict. He was given his first taste of heroin by an American traveler ten years ago. He says that every morning he goes down to the temple of the living goddess "to get power so I don't have to use this heroin." But every afternoon he returns to Freak Street to get high. Is there a Freak Street in your life? Is there a Freak Street where every day you get up and you begin to agonize that you'll not have to do down and spend the day on Freak Street? Maybe your addiction is not heroin or some kind of a drug, but your visit to Freak Street might be coming from a variety of reasons. Well, this one boy went and prayed to a false god to get him off of Freak Street. He'd pray in the morning, but every afternoon he would be on Freak Street.

I want to give you a positive word on how to get off of Freak Street. You come to Jesus, and the Bible says that Jesus will make out of you a new creature. You can be a new creature in Christ Jesus. You don't have to live your life on Freak Street; you can be set free, and be freed up to be the man or woman that God wants you to be. Why spend your whole life on Freak Street? Be free in Jesus. *"Therefore if any man is in Christ, he is a new creature; the old things passed away; behold, all things are become new."* II Corinthians 5:17.

† † †

YOUR ATTITUDE WILL DETERMINE HOW OLD YOU ARE

An old gentleman sat down on a park bench one day, looking very lonely and dejected. Seeing the old man sitting there, another person felt compassionate toward him and sat down beside him. When he asked what was wrong, the old man replied, "I guess I'm just getting old."

The person responded, "Oh, you having rheumatism?"

"No," replied the old man. "Worse than that . . . I'm having reminiscences."

The old gentleman certainly exemplifies the characteristics of many who find themselves "getting older." However, I know many people who suffer the same kind of trauma, the same kind of "reminiscences," and they're not 70, 80, or 90 years old; many are in their 20's, 30's and 40's. The Minnesota State Medical Association released an interesting statement the other day that accurately depicts many of these people. According to the statement, "Some are elderly at 40, others young at 80; but you are genuinely old if you feel that tomorrow holds no promise; you take no interest in the activities of youth; and you long for the 'good old days,' feeling that they were the best."

It's not the number of years we've lived, but our attitude as we face each day that determines how we live. The Psalmist said that in old age we "will flourish like the palm tree," and that we "shall bring forth fruit in old age" (Psalm 92:12, 14). The spirit within us does not grow old. The aging process can bring wrinkles and can certainly slow us down, but when we maintain a positive attitude, viewing each day as a gift from God, we won't grow old inside. The brow might wrinkle, but you choose whether or not the spirit will "wrinkle." The legs might get a little slower, but the attitude can speed up as we begin to look at each day as a fresh, new challenge. The eyes might begin to grow dim, and even require that you use bifocals, but the spirit's eye can always be 20/20.

Some people are elderly at 40, but some of the youngest people I know are 80. Your attitude will determine how old you are. It just depends on you.

ALONE BUT NOT LONELY

It has been reported that loneliness can create a serious health problem. Millions of Americans suffer from depression, anxiety and fatigue that are linked to loneliness. In one nationwide study, 22 percent of the population said they felt, "Lonely or remote from other people." In another poll taken by *Psychology Today,* loneliness was the most frequent problem mentioned. Thirty-eight percent of female and forty-three percent of male readers said they often felt lonely.

People who live alone tend to say they are lonely more frequently than people living with others. Since surveys reportedly show that there is an increasing number of Americans who live alone, we can infer that the frequency of loneliness is increasing. In 1940 only eight percent of American households contained one person. In 1980, 22 percent of households contained only one person.

We know that severe loneliness can lead to a variety of problems. One recent study showed that among divorced men the death rate due to heart disease was twice the rate for married men. This suggests that living alone and feeling lonely may actually create very serious health problems.

There was a man in the Bible who knew what it meant to be alone. His name was John and he was placed in exile on the Isle of Patmos. From reading John's letter it can be noted that John was alone but he was not lonely. He had a companion and that companion was the presence of the Spirit of Christ. Jesus said, *"I will never leave you and I will never forsake you."*

Just as John learned that truth that was to cure him of loneliness, thus you and I can find the same Companion that can cure our loneliness. He will be with us regardless of the hour of the day or night. He will comfort us with His presence regardless of our circumstances and in and through Him we can learn the difference between being alone and being lonely.

"THE BURNOUT SYNDROME"

Psychologists are greatly convinced about a growing number of individuals who are experiencing emotional and professional burnout. It has been suggested that 94 percent of all U.S. organizations are patterned to set up a "burnout syndrome" in their employees. Burnout is marked by a severe depletion of physical, spiritual, and emotional energy. Moreover it manifests itself by emotional exhaustion, negative attitudes, personal devaluation and a feeling that the individual has little effect on the overall product or service.

Burnout is also recognized as a major job hazard. One counselor estimates that it attacks 85 percent of all professional people at some time or another. Burnout is not just limited to secular employees, but it also invades the ranks of ministers and other religious workers. These, too, are not exempt from burnout.

Now, what can be done as a preventive measure? One thing is that our emotional reserves must not be depleted by continuously putting out more than we take in. Jesus often got away from the stress of His ministry and spent long hours in prayer with His Father. When the disciples of Jesus returned from their first preaching mission, they excitedly reported all that they had done and taught. Then, because so many people were coming and going that they did not even have a chance to eat, He said to them, *"Come with me by yourselves to a quiet place and get some rest."* (Mark 8:30-31)

As we move in the business of life from day to day, we must realize the dangers of burnout syndrome. Can it be overcome? Yes, when we listen to the words of Jesus and learn to come aside, be by ourselves, and simply rest awhile.

✝ ✝ ✝

THE CUTTING EDGE

As a boy growing up, it was my responsibility to make sure that there was always "coal and kindling" in the house for the coal heater. Every afternoon I had to make sure that the coal bucket was filled and the kindling cut and stacked by the bucket so the fire could be started the next morning. When the time came each day to bring in the coal and cut the kindling, I would often have much rather been out playing. On one particular day, when I was out playing football with the rest of the boys, I was called in to do my chores. I got extremely angry because I was having fun playing and now I had to stop and do something I didn't want to do. I got ready to chop the wood and jerked up the old yard ax, only to watch the ax head fly off the handle. Now that really made me angry. As anger and frustration swelled up in me, I just started chopping away at an old piece of wood with nothing more than the ax handle. I didn't cut any kindling; all I did was burn up a lot of energy, because I was cutting with only the handle, not the ax.

In life we are beset by interruptions and obstacles, bringing about in us anger and frustration. We begin to chop away at life with nothing more than an ax handle. There's not the cutting edge of spiritual life within us that will enable us to "cut it" in life. We must learn that the cutting edge is on the head and not the handle. You can take the handle and work as long and as hard as you want, but you won't get the job done. It requires the cutting edge. How sharp is the spiritual ax that you have? How sharp is the cutting edge in your life spiritually? The cutting edge of a spiritual life will enable you to "cut it" in life, and not just burn up energy.

† † †

"MAKE PEACE AND RETAIN INNER CALM"

When Leonardo da Vinci was painting his great masterpiece entitled "The Last Supper," he became filled with hot anger with a friend. He lashed out at this friend with bitter and stinging words. He was so filled with anger that he actually threatened his friend with vengeance.

After this unpleasant encounter with his friend, da Vinci returned to his canvas to continue the masterpiece. With the strokes of the brush he began to paint the face of Jesus. He found, however, that he was so disturbed and disquieted within that his composure was gone. His work was suffering because of the inner sufferings. After identifying the problem, he went out immediately and sought his friend and humbly asked his friend for forgiveness.

Now, having solved the problem that he had with his friend, he returned to his great masterpiece with an inner calm. He was then enabled to give the Master's face the tender and delicate expression he knew that it must have.

The uncontrolled tongue can become an instrument of bitterness or an instrument of blessing. The Bible says in James 3:5, *"Even so the tongue is a little member, and boasteth great things. Behold, how great a matter a little fire kindleth."*

There are times when the inner storms rage within us and can only be stilled by confessing to that friend, family member, or loved one that our words were hurtful and we are sorry. Then we can return with an inner calm to today's tasks.

† † †

BE CONTENT WITH YOUR LIFE

Believe it or not, the average American is exposed to about 300 advertisements each day. The "Madison Avenue Pied Piper" is constantly leading us about, creating a world of exaggeration, and convincing us that to live without the latest product -- the newest and most improved -- is not really living at all. It's not only the big, expensive purchases the advertisements are prompting you to buy, they are aimed at every aspect of our lives, from new cars to liver pills.

Whatever the product, the basic idea they're selling is that we should never be content. In the eyes of the advertisements, to be satisfied with what we have or what we are is wrong. Our clothes shouldn't be white, they should be whiter than white. The same old candy bar we've eaten for years isn't good enough, there's something new on the market. The list goes on and on. They even bombard us with comments and insinuations about ourselves. We don't look good enough, . . . we don't even smell good enough.

So where does all of this lead us? Well, it's good in the sense that it's "The American Way." It's so much a part of our economy that it has become an extremely profitable, $14 billion a year business. Yet there is another side. John D. Rockefeller was once asked how much it takes to satisfy a man. His wise reply was, "A little more than he has." When we're bombarded an estimated 300 times each day by advertisements that are telling us that we need more or that in some way, we're just not quite good enough, we can become very discontent with ourselves and our lives. This can lead to feelings of inadequacy, unhappiness, and eventually to a negative self-image.

How do we combat these 300 subtle -- and not so subtle -- suggestions each day? There is a way to overcome the power of suggestion that they possess and gain inner strength and satisfaction in your life. The Bible teaches in Philippians 4:11-12:

> "I have learned to be content in whatever circumstances I am. I know how to get along with humble means, and I also know how to live in prosperity; in any and every circumstance I have learned the secret of being filled and of going hungry, both of having abundance, and suffering need."

The Apostle Paul had learned that the "good life" comes through a balanced life; that contentment does not come from your circumstances but from within. The "Madison Avenue Pied Piper" would convince you of just the opposite -- and to believe that will turn your life into an "emotional yoyo." You don't have to live like that. The Bible will show you how to be content with your life.

BALLOONS OR BLESSINGS?

"Six Flags" is open again! As I drove by the amusement park the other day, I began to recall some of my experiences there. We lived in South Carolina when my children were small, and it was necessary for me to drive all the way to Atlanta to go to "Six Flags." We would get up early in the morning and begin our journey. Inevitably, the day we picked would turn out to be the hottest day of the year, and for some reason, everybody in Georgia would show up on that day!

Now, I've never been a "Six Flags" enthusiast. You see, I really just do not enjoy riding a roller coaster, I don't enjoy being dropped through the air in a parachute, and I can think of better ways to get soaking wet than plunging along in a hollowed out "log" on the "log ride." But being a loyal, loving father, I would find myself, once again, at the "Six Flags" gate, handing over hard-earned cash to buy tickets.

First we would have to stand in line just to get inside the park. Then we would go from ride to ride, waiting through endless lines of marching people. They aren't just long, straight lines, where you can see what you're getting into before you enter. They are actually quite misleading. You get in a line thinking, "This isn't so bad," but soon realize the crowds aren't simply moving forward. You go back and forth -- I always feel as though I'm pacing in slow motion -- and about the time you decide the line is too long to wait through, well, there's no way out. You're stuck in the middle of all those people with no choice but to wait . . . and wait . . . and wait. Supposedly the lines are made that way to create the illusion that you're moving faster. It doesn't work for me. An hour is an hour, whether I'm walking in a straight line or back and forth.

Well, after one of our all day excursions, we packed everyone back into the car and headed home. I was feeling tired and thinking about all of the money we spent buying tickets and food -- hot dogs, ice cream, the whole bit, and believed that everyone was asleep but me. From the back seat came the sound of a little sniffle. As it grew louder and louder, I looked back and there was my youngest daughter, beginning to whine. Finally after I asked what was wrong for the third time, she burst into tears and said it . . . she didn't get a balloon at "Six Flags."

That did it. It was more than I could handle. In a loud, very stern voice, I reminded her of all the things we had done that day, of how much money Daddy had spent, how tired I was, and that I really didn't enjoy being there in the first place. After all of that, she was crying because she didn't get a balloon?

By that time, everyone in the car was awake. My wife leaned over and settled me down, and we promised our little daughter that the next time we visited "Six Flags," she would get a balloon.

Having recently been reminded of that experience, I couldn't help comparing it to the way we so often treat God. We enjoy many of the blessings of God, but we often don't stop to thank Him for those blessings. What we end up doing is crying and complaining because we didn't get a "balloon." We forget all of the things we have, and see only the thing we wanted, but didn't get. Maybe it's time we learned to focus on all of the blessings of the Lord instead of whining over the "balloon" we didn't get.

† † †

DON'T LET PAST MISTAKES BIND YOU

One of the key ingredients for success in any endeavor is the ability to put your mistakes behind you. The reason many people fail in their climb to the top of the ladder is that they allow their mistakes to become a psychological chain that holds them to the bottom. Some of these psychological chains are put around us as children, others are placed on us as we become teenagers or young adults. The remarkable thing about these chains is that many are never broken, . . . they bind for a lifetime.

Some of the mistakes that bind our lives are personal, and

unique only to us, while others are common mistakes that are made by many people each day. However, the fact that these mistakes are common to many does not make them less difficult to handle. In a book dealing with applied psychology, the results of a study that involved asking 500 businessmen about the greatest mistake they ever made listed some interesting statements. The list of greatest mistakes included some specific mistakes, but it also listed those below, which are of a broader nature.

1. Worrying about things that cannot be changed.
2. Failing to live within my income.
3. Believeing that success is measured by wealth.
4. Forcing my thoughts and attitudes on others.
5. Forgetting that the best way to get even is to forgive and forget.
6. Refusing to put aside trivials in order to accomplish a greater good.
7. Reading worthless books and magazines.
8. Lack of life purpose.
9. Thinking that others can't get along without me.
10. Failing to remember that God is aware of my life.

Having read this list, we can't help but wonder what 10 mistakes we would list for our own lives. Thinking about those mistakes, we need to ask ourselves, do they continue to wrap around us as chains, keeping us from being all that God wants us to be, and doing all that God wants us to do?

A Bible verse that long ago became one of my favorites speaks of having to recognize my past failures and past mistakes, and "forgetting those things which are behind . . ." (Phil. 3:13). We need to learn how to have a "big forgetter," because if we don't forget, rest assured that our past mistakes will serve to keep us in chains, and will bind us all of our lives. The key that will unlock the chains is learning how to "forget the things which are behind," so that our lives can be based on the present day.

2
The Way of the Family

IN THIS CHAPTER . . . .

I Don't Love You Anymore
Principles For Strong Families
How You Say It Makes A Difference
What Is The Most Important Thing In The World?
Pulling Together Keeps The Bells Ringing
Violence In The Home
Men's Lib
Taking Stock
Come Dine With Me
Family Prayer
Begin At Home
Young People Get Big Bucks
"The Cost Of Raising A Child"
Pedal Together
Learn To Back Up In Your Relationships
Memories
There's Just No Place Like Home
How God Meets Our Needs
Let The Feelings You Pass To Your Children Be Positive

I DON'T LOVE YOU ANYMORE

Love isn't static. Love will either grow or it will begin to dwindle. The love of a person who has been married for fifty years will not be the same as when he was first married. When he said "I do," he probably really meant it (according to the level of his understanding). However, fifty years later his love has grown stronger -- or weaker.

When a young couple say their wedding vows they have happy visions of years to come. They will gladly make sacrifices for each other and seek to serve each other's needs in total unselfishness.

This kind of love can begin to grow and mature through the years. And love which has matured through years of self-giving is much more beautiful than that "first love."

There is another side to this story, though. Many people live not in making sacrifices, but in selfishness in their relationship with each other. Selfishness can cause love to begin to wither and even to die.

This certainly occurred to the children of Israel in the Bible. When they were rescued from Egypt they loved God like a new bride loves her husband. He was the center of their lives and they were very faithful to Him. But after a while that love began to cool, and soon they committed spiritual adultery by worshipping heathen gods. Their glow for God was gone.

Be totally honest with yourself. Do you love the Lord God more or less today than when you said "I do" to Him?

† † †

PRINCIPLES FOR STRONG FAMILIES

If there is a segment of society today that lives underneath tremendous stress, it is the family. Homes are constantly being broken up all across America. Many homes that stay together simply do so for convenience sake; people live together under the same roof but they know nothing of a stable, active home and family life. There is a constant cry for HELP to begin to establish themselves as a complete unit. Let me suggest five principles that will help you to build a strong, stable family base.

First, learn to show appreciation for every member of the family. Strong families build one upon the other. It's so easy to tear down one another rather than build up. Learn to show appreciation. Learn to say words like, "thank you," "you look great today," and "I love you." Secondly, learn to spend time together. As a family, this is a vital foundational principle. Talk to one another or *do* things together! Spending time is not sitting around every day staring at the tube!

Principle number three: be committed to build a strong family. Strong families do not "just happen." Strong families are built. They're determined to make it work. Be committed to the commitment of a strong family. Another principle is -- be selfless. Strong families learn how to try to bless one another. Families that constantly fail are built on their own selfish egos. One final principle -- love unconditionally. Strong families have learned that principle. The roof that covers all other principles is the roof of love. As you build your house, the foundation should be Jesus. Then the four walls are added. These four walls would be the four principles that I've listed above. The roof that covers the foundation and the walls is the roof of love. Just learn to love one another unconditionally.

When a hit record is produced, the record industry can put almost anything on the flip side. They know that what will sell the record will be the hit side of the record. Remember that when you were married, you got the hit side. You saw all of the advantages and all of the good, outstanding qualities; but along with the hit side there came the flip side. The flip side are those negative aspects that all of us contain. Only unconditional love will be the kind of love that will supercede the hit side as well as the flip side.

HOW YOU SAY IT MAKES A DIFFERENCE

An elderly couple who could neither read nor write had early in their lives decided that their son would have a college education. This became one of their life's goals. As their boy grew up, it became apparent that he had a lot of abilities and was very intelligent. His parents were extremely proud of him, and were overcome with joy when the day finally arrived for him to go to college. While he was away at school, they eagerly looked forward to receiving his letters, and would ask a neighbor to read them as soon as they arrived.

One day the old dad received a letter from his son. Anxious to hear what his boy had written, he stopped a neighbor who was rushing by, and asked him if he would take just a minute to read the letter. Irritated by the interruption, the neighbor took the letter and very rapidly read through it, as though he were reading a newscast. In the last paragraph the boy wrote, "Dad, I need some money. Could you send me some at once?" Well, the way the neighbor read it made the request sound like a demand, and the dad didn't like it at all.

But as the dad continued walking down the road, he couldn't stop thinking about his son's letter. Before long, another neighbor came walking leisurely by, and the dad asked him if he had time to read it to him. The neighbor responded that he had plenty of time, and would enjoy it. He began reading the letter very thoughtfully, and with much feeling. When he came to the last paragraph, he read in a soft voice, "Dad, I need some money. Could you send me some at once?"

The old dad stood there wiping away his tears, and said, "Now, that's more like it. When he asks like that, he can get every cent I have."

The same words, but with different inflections, make all the difference in the world. You know, it's not only what we say, but how we say it that is important. The next time you're in a hurry, and someone stops you to ask a question, remember that the person asking will hear how you say the words as clearly as the words you say, and it could make a difference in his whole day. *"A soft voice turneth away wrath"* (Proverbs 15:1).

WHAT IS THE MOST IMPORTANT WORD IN THE WORLD?

Many people would say that the most important word in the world, apart from a proper name, would be a word like "parents", "child," "son," "daughter," or "love." But what about the word "relationship"? Where would any of the above be without that most important word, relationship? Relationship is the track that all of the others operate on.

Maybe a little reflection will help to expand upon this word relationship. Think of the many crises that you've experienced during your lifetime:

As a little child, when you became separated from your mom in the supermarket . . .

When you were a child, and wanted to go out to play, but your parents said "no" . . .

When you were a teenager, and your sweetheart had just broken your heart by breaking up with you . . .

Or perhaps you've experienced the pain of the death of a parent or spouse.

The list is an inexhaustible one. But now consider the warm and wonderful times of your life. The giggles and laughter of little children as they ran barefoot through the house . . . the thrill of your first date, or the enthusiasm you felt when your boyfriend brought you your first corsage. And what about the time during which you and your husband were engaged, the date of your marriage, and the sound of the instruments when they began to play, "Here Comes the Bride"?

What one characteristic runs through all of these experiences, both good and bad? The word relationship. You see, if you solve the relationship problems, there will be no divorce, no war, no employer-employee problems. Solve the relationship problem, and you'll solve even the most perplexing problems that man will ever face.

If you find your life in turmoil today, it might be because of a ruptured relationship. Jesus commented on that when He said If *"thy brother hath aught against thee . . . go thy way and be reconciled to thy brother"* (Matthew 5:23, 24).

PULLING TOGETHER KEEPS THE BELLS RINGING

A young couple married not long ago in a beautiful, country church wedding ceremony. The weddings in that church were just a little different from other church weddings. At the end of the ceremony, the old preacher would say, "It is traditional in our church for the bride to ring the church bell before leaving." The beautiful young bride was escorted back to where the big church bell hung overhead, and pulled the rope that would make the bell ring. Not a sound came from the belfry. She pulled again and again, but still the bell didn't ring. The young bride was becoming quite embarrassed, and although she tried as hard as she could, the bell simply would not ring.

The wise old preacher, seeing her frustration and embarrassment, finally signaled for the bridegroom to help her. The bridegroom raced to the side of his bride, grabbed hold of the rope, and they both pulled the rope with all of their strength. Their combined effort made the bell ring out, and the sound of the bell ringing could be heard over the whole community.

The old preacher walked over to the young people, and said, "You know, married life is like ringing that bell . . . it's much easier when the two of you pull together."

In a marriage union, it is extremely important that both husband and wife seek to "pull together." This pulling together would lead them to seek to please each other and to seek God's blessings on their home. Part of doing that is learning to overlook the faults of the other person. The old evangelist, Billy Sunday, used to say, "Try praising your wife, men, even if it does frighten her at first!" And that's good advice! When we begin to pull together, we'll find that the bells begin to ring for us.

You made certain commitments at the wedding altar. Have the years eroded part of those commitments? Perhaps you need to ask yourself how often you've helped "ring the bell" in the life of your marriage partner. Maybe the bell hasn't rung in a while. It's time to grab hold of the rope and pull . . . together, and you'll discover that the sounds of the bell will still ring out. The Lord tells us in Mark 10:8 that when two people marry, *"The two shall become one . . ."* When we work together as one, pulling together, everything becomes much easier.

VIOLENCE IN THE HOME

PSYCHOLOGY Professor Ellen Berscheid of the University of Minnesota, is quoted in *Parade Magazine* as saying: "Americans have a greater chance of encountering violence in their own families than in dark streets and dangerous neighborhoods." She cites a series of studies, headed by New Hampshire Family Psychologist Murray Straus, of 2000 families in the United States and found the following: (1) One in six couples experience physical violence from a spouse. (2) Six out of every 100 husbands and wives, some three million homes, were involved in serious acts such as kicking, punching, hitting with an object, or using a knife or gun. (3) Fourteen of every one hundred children suffered physical abuse from parents. (4) More than half of all children suffered attacks from brothers or sisters.

These alarming statistics abruptly awaken us again to the awesome need of establishing and building our home upon the proper foundation of Christian principles. The one solution for violence in the home is for that home to be built upon the solid foundation of Christ. Love can permeate the home and be the controlling emotion rather than frustration, bitterness and violence.

"And the rain descended, and the floods came, and the winds blew, and beat upon that house; and it fell not: for it was founded upon a rock." (Matthew 7:25)

† † †

MEN'S LIB

One of the most popular controversies of our day is the idea of what a man should be . . . a "real man." One notion is that men need to "get in touch" with themselves, and develop their "tenderness and nurturing" qualities.

According to Philadelphia psychologist John D. Franklin, the trouble with that idea is that some men, in trying to become "nurturing fathers," have given up their "power and strength as men, and have shifted their identity away from functioning in the world and toward being overly receptive to the demands of the home, overly receptive to mothering. This imbalance has created a weak male figure, one who has become more of a mother than the mother ever was." The psychologist summed it up by saying that some men, in trying to be what society dictates they should be have simply become "wimpy."

It just seems that men are having a difficult time finding a balance. The pendulum either swings too far one way or the other, and the man becomes "wimpy" or believes that he has to have some type of "macho" image to prove his masculinity.

Isn't it enough for a man that he be what God intended for him to be . . . a loving provider-protector for his wife and children? Is it not enough for him, in his own personal identity, to be able to embrace his son and daughter and say to them, "I love you," or to express his love for his wife and still maintain that role which God outlined for him in the Bible? Can he not look upon himself as being the loving provider-protector for his family, instead of relying upon the world to provide the standard by which he measures his masculinity?

A man can find his own, individual identity in a personal walk with God. When he begins to see himself in this light -- as God intended for him to be -- he begins to make an impact, not only in his family, but also in his community.

A man is not a man simply because he can unbutton his shirt down to his belt buckle, nor does he become a man by losing his individual identity -- giving up his power and strength as a man to fit into the mold which much of society dictates. As the Philadelphia psychologist contends, "A man is a man when he finds himself grounded in his personal commitment to a caring God, and then has this commitment flow out of him to a personal commitment to his family that he will be their loving provider-protector." In that, he can see himself as being a success in life. When he has become that person which God intended for him to be, then and only then is he truly liberated.

† † †

TAKING STOCK

It's been a long time since you took stock of where you're going, hasn't it? How about an evaluation of the kids? Or your marriage? Or your own personal future? You know what I mean. Trimming off the fat of lazy thinking and taking a lean hard look at the years that are ahead of you. Have you ever stopped long enough to let the reality really grab you?

When you begin to consider your own family in the next decade where will you be and what will you be doing? If you think about it, there will be some things that seem impossible. As I reflect back, it seems like just the other day when our home was a cross between Grand Central Station, the Indianapolis 500 and the San Diego Zoo! All three of the children were at home and growing up; but now they're grown, they're establishing lives and careers of their own and now home is not like Grand Central Station or the Indianapolis 500 and not even like the San Diego Zoo. Sometimes it just gets too quiet!

It's important to set aside time for evaluation and a regrouping of your thoughts. Even the sports world has a time out in the seventh inning stretch, a pit stop and a half time! Force yourself to pull off the road, get off the fast lane, put your pace in neutral and begin to ask yourself some hard questions. For instance, am I really happy? . . . genuinely challenged and fulfilled in life? Is the direction of my life now leading me toward a satisfying and rewarding future? Can I honestly say that I am in the nucleus of God's will for me? What about the kids . . . is sufficient time being spent with the children so that they know that I love them and care very much for them and about their future? Am I communicating life's goals, a proper value system, a standard of moral purity, a desire for excellence and a commitment to loyalty, integrity, generosity and honesty to my children? Do they really know how I feel about these things? Are they aware that they are worthwhile and valuable? Are they growing up to be positive, confident, secure, highly esteemed young men and young women? When they leave the nest will they be able to stand alone?

For what are you asking the Lord on behalf of yourself and your children? I want to challenge you to stop long enough to think it over. Don't just think, but get alone and write down your thoughts, your dreams, your aspirations. Refuse to let tonight's television program or some insignificant activity interrupt this necessary discipline.

You know, home is a lot of things . . . but mainly it is the place where life makes up its mind. As you think on these things and follow through with the necessary changes that will enable you to accomplish your plans, you'll find that life can get back on target and, best of all, you'll be able to say, "I have not lived in vain."

† † †

COME DINE WITH ME

It would start the very first of the week. My mama would warn me, "Now you get ready because the Preacher's coming on Sunday!" My parents counted it an honor to have the preacher come to visit for Sunday afternoon dinner.

I was instructed to put on my best behaviour and lectured to from Monday to Sunday afternoon on how to conduct myself! Sunday dinner always consisted of fried chicken, assorted vegetables, potato salad, and Merita plain cake for dessert.

The preacher would come after the Sunday morning service. He would be greeted by everyone and he in turn would greet everyone. He would be ushered in to the dinner table and have the honor of sitting at the head, and, of course, always lead the prayer. In those days the children always waited to eat until after the adults were through. I remember now waiting in the back room until the preacher finished dinner. The preacher would eat for what seemed like all afternoon and then he would enter into a conversation with my daddy. They would talk . . . and talk . . . and talk . . . and talk! I did not dare to stick my head in the door because I knew if I showed any signs of being impatient my dad would "apply the board of education to my seat of learning!"

Finally, they would leave the table and go into the sitting room, signaling that it was time for me to eat. I looked at what was left over from that chicken -- all that I saw was a neck, a back and a wing. As I reflect on it now as a man, what was left were the remains no one else wanted. I was confronted with left-overs!

I learned my lesson, now that I'm a preacher, and I'm glad we feed the children first and get them out of the way, for it helps me to overcome my "psychological hang-ups" from my childhood of having to digress on all that the preacher did by eating all the chicken at dinner time! When I sat down at the table, it seemed that the table was almost empty. I'm reminded now of another table -- a table that is set by the Master.

When Jesus said, *"Behold I stand at the door and knock. If any man will hear my voice and open the door, I will come in to sup with him and he with me."* I'm aware that when I invite Christ in, He enters in as the guest. After entering as the guest, He suddenly becomes the host. As the host, He always invites me to the scrumptuous table that He offers.

The world beckons me to come and eat of the garbage can of this life. Jesus says come and dine, the table is full and scrumptuous. I'd much rather eat from His table. The food is much better from the Lord's table than from the garbage can of the world, and there are never, never any "left-overs."

† † †

FAMILY PRAYER

There was a plaque in our house that stated that a family that prays together, stays together. The first national study of the impact of religion on family stability concludes that the family that prays together really does stay together. Husbands and wives who consider themselves very religious and attend services nearly every week are 42% more likely to be in their first marriage than those who never attend services.

Religious commitment does not necessarily insure marital bliss. Those survey respondents who said they frequently attend religious services did not report that their marriages were any happier than the marriages of those who attend infrequently or not at all. But those with very strong attachments to their religions were 23% more likely to report very happy marriages than those who had no attachment. It does stress that the family that does pray together does stay together.

† † †

BEGIN AT HOME

President Reagan recently stressed that the Nation's schools "need to restore good, old fashioned discipline." Our President asked the justice and education departments to "find ways we can help teachers and administrators enforce discipline."

Well, I've got a suggestion to help the President find a way to help teachers. I believe that it's time to recognize that discipline does not begin in the classroom, discipline does not begin in the church, discipline begins at home. Our President stated that "in too many schools across the land, teachers can't teach because they lack the authority to make students take tests and hand in homework." Our President said, whatever it takes we must make certain that American schools are temples of learning and not drug dens.

Well, the point to begin is in the home. It is high time that parents realized that the discipline problem is not in the hands of the school teacher, it's in the hands of the parents, and we are commissioned by God to discipline the children. In Ephesians chapter 6, *"children, obey your parents in the Lord, for this is right."* I believe you'll find it true that if discipline is stressed at home, it'll be exemplified in the classroom. Mr. President, the way to help our schools is to restore discipline in the home.

YOUNG PEOPLE GET BIG BUCKS

Today's teenagers have some big bucks! This is a conclusion reached through a survey conducted by Simmons Market Research. The survey found that the combined incomes of people between the ages of 12 and 19 totaled some 600 million dollars per week. Sixty percent of these young people received that income from part-time or full-time jobs. Now, tack on to that an estimated 80 million dollars a week in allowances, and that brings the total teen income to around 35 billion dollars a year.

Another survey, reported in "Changing Times" magazine by Road Youth Poll, found that teenagers spent a record 42.6 billion dollars in 1981. Some of the things purchased included food, clothing, movies, cars, cosmetics, records, tapes and stereos.

If you don't think that youth is big money business, then examine some of the commercials you see on television. Pay attention to the specific age group that the commercials aim at. The big money in youth is there, and the merchants are out to get it.

With as much money as teenagers make -- and as much as they spend -- you would probably feel safe in drawing the conclusion that teenagers ought to be happy. However, it's a frightening reality that over one million of these teenagers will run away from home this year, and that 3.3 million teenagers between the age of 14 and 17 have become problem drinkers. The thing that becomes glaringly obvious to me is this: with the record 42.6 billion dollars spent by teenagers in 1981, they were not able to buy inward peace and inward happiness. You see, the thing that many, many people today fail to realize is that inward peace and happiness is something that is not bought with dollars. It's not purchased as a product. It won't be reported in "Changing Times." Inward peace comes only when you know the Prince of Peace, *"For He Himself is our peace . . ."* (Ephesians 2:14).

† † †

"THE COST OF RAISING A CHILD"

The family economics research group of the United States Department of Agriculture informs us that it now costs $65,000 to rear a child from birth to age 18. Now, I thought that would get your attention!

According to their research, a parent can plan on spending $15,160.75 for feeding each child at home and $1,763.00 for buying the child meals away from home. It was computed that $5,194.50 will be spent on clothing the child, and, in addition, the housing cost of raising a child will exceed $21,000.00. On top of all this, medical care can be expected to be almost $3,500.00, while public school costs will be approximately $1,121.00. And don't forget to add in transportation costs which may cost you $10,000.00. Finally, included in the total cost figure is $7,731.00 that is classified as "incidentals."

Now, that is quite a financial investment to make in one child! Children were once considered an asset, but now are a financial liability. Parents will usually go out of their way to make the financial investment for their child, but will often fail to invest in their child's spiritual well-being. The spiritual investment is summarized in the scripture that says, *"Train up a child in the way he should go, and when he is old he will not depart from it"* (Proverbs 22:6).

This spiritual investment in a child will also "cost" the parents. It will "cost" the parents because of their responsibility of setting the example through their personal commitment to the Lord. To make this spiritual investment, the parents themselves must walk in fellowship with the Lord.

After making this spiritual investment in their child, what is a parent going to get in return? When do the dividends come in? Quite simply, when you hear these words, "Mom and Dad, I love you!" Also, your reward will be great when you watch your child grow in his or her own personal relationship with the Lord. Then, the $65,000 plus your spiritual investment reaps its greatest dividends!

PEDAL TOGETHER

Two boys happened upon a bicycle built for two. They decided to go for a ride, so the first boy got on the front seat, and the other took the back. Before they'd gone very far they came to a hill. The boy on front pedaled as hard as he could to get up that hill, almost to the point of sheer exhaustion. Finally he made it to the top, and had to stop to rest. As he got off the bike, he looked into the eyes of his buddy, and with perspiration literally dropping off his face, said, "I thought we never would reach the top of this hill!" He got the shock of his life when his buddy exclaimed, "We never would have either, if I hadn't held on the brake and kept us from rolling back down!"

The story of these two boys illustrates why we are often unable to reach the top in the quality of our home life. As married couples we often find ourselves in that kind of situation. One seems to want to pedal, while the other desires to keep on the brake. And if we ever do reach the top, we find ourselves in sheer exhaustion, not having enjoyed the ride. You can't ride a bicycle built for two with one pedaling and the other holding the brake on, and you can't build a satisfactory marriage using the same philosophy. It will take both who are willing to pedal; both who have the desire to reach the top of the hill. When both are willing to pedal, we move up faster, we move up with more joy, and we move up . . . with a whole lot less exhaustion.

As we strive to build our Christian families, let's remind ourselves that there is a seat on the bicycle for all of us, and we all have to do our share of the pedaling. You don't coast up the hill, you have to work at it. But when you get to the top, and can see the view from there, you'll find that the ride going up -- building your family -- was worth the trip.

† † †

LEARN TO BACK UP IN YOUR RELATIONSHIPS

A man who had just purchased a new automobile eagerly got into his car and prepared to drive home. To avoid paying freight costs, he had arranged to pick the new car up at the dock in one of our coastal cities. There were no salesmen around to answer questions, and no instructions in the car, but he wasn't worried. He knew how to drive, and figured that was all he needed to know.

Around lunch time the man was becoming a little hungry, and decided to stop at a restaurant for lunch. When he finished eating, he got back into his car and started the ignition, ready to continue on home. Much to his surprise, he discovered that he could not find the reverse gear. He worked and worked, but still was unable to find it. Finally, he got out of the car, put it into neutral, and pushed it out into the street so that he was able to just go forward and continue on his way.

Well, the car really did have a reverse gear, but the man couldn't find it. No one would be willing to buy a car that didn't have a reverse gear, even if the manufacturer was willing to knock a thousand dollars off the sticker price. You just wouldn't want it. Unfortunately though, a lot of people who wouldn't think of investing in a car that didn't have a reverse gear would invest their lives in a relationship where there seems to be no reverse. They try to conduct human relations without the will to back up or go in reverse for the sake of harmony. Marriages break up, friendships are separated and churches fall apart simply because stubborn people won't back up. We dig our feet into the ground and refuse to ever give in, to ever say things like, "I'm sorry," or "I was wrong," or "It's my fault. Why don't we just start all over again?"

The Bible identifies these destructive behavioral traits of stubbornness and pride, and warns us that *"pride goes before the destruction, and a haughty spirit before the fall"* (Proverbs 16:18). This Bible passage simply implies that you need a reverse in your relationships as much as you need one in your car.

MEMORIES

I was born in the back room of an old mill house in South Carolina, the son of a textile mill couple. That old house had real high ceilings, and it was build on what we called "brick pillows," and had nothing underpinning it. The lights hung down on long cords in the middle of the rooms, and you'd have to go in at night and feel your way to the center of the room, reaching out for the light. Finally you'd touch the string, pull it, and the light would come on.

In the winter the only room we heated was the back room, and it was heated with a coal heater. Sometimes the other rooms would get so cold that ice would form on the insides of the windows. You'd curl up in bed at night with layers and layers of quilts stacked on top of you, and once you were settled in, you dared not get up until early the next morning. Then you'd jump out of bed and make a bee-line to the back room where the coal heater was.

The day finally arrived when urban renewal moved into the neighborhood. All of the old houses were being torn down, and mom and dad were one of the last families to leave. I tried to explain to them that they were getting a much, much, nicer house. They would have carpet on all the floors, lower ceilings, and every room would be heated. It would just be an ideal place to live, and the house had already been purchased and was ready for them to move in.

As they were getting ready to leave, I stood in the backyard with my father, trying once again to comfort him by explaining how much better off they were going to be. Finally he stopped me and said, "But you don't understand, son. You see that tree over there? Your brother helped me plant that tree. And do you see that tree over there, behind the house? You stood beside me as I planted that tree, when you were just a boy." On and on he talked, pointing out things that would bring memories back to him, memories of his family, memories that meant something.

Only then did I realize that in the heart and mind of this old man, it was not the thought of the new house that grieved him, it was the thought of leaving behind the home where so many memories had been made . . . memories of his children, memories of his joys, and his sorrows. Solomon wrote in Proverbs 10:7, *"the memory of the just is blessed . . ."* Make sure your memories count.

† † †

THERE'S JUST NO PLACE LIKE HOME

B.J. Thomas sings my kind of tune when he strums the chords to "Home Where I Belong." You can tell the guy's been on the road a lot when he sings lines like this . . . "When I'm feeling lonely and when I'm feeling blue, it's such a joy to know that I'm only passing through. I'm headed home, I'm going home where I belong." The simple truth is that there is no place like home. No place! There never will be. Be it ever so humble, it is still home -- no scene any more beautiful than one step inside the front door. Anyone who loves his family, and treasures his time around the supper table, followed by a couple of hours of just being arm in arm with his "gang" in the den can certainly reaffirm that.

Recently I was traveling in the beautiful southwestern part of the United States, just out of Abilene, Texas. The country was really beautiful, but you know, it didn't compare with our beautiful southeast Atlanta. The reason is that this is home. I was up in the beautiful coastal area of South Carolina a couple of weeks later, but still, there is just something about coming home. Even when I travel to areas that are considered to be glamourous and exciting, they just can't compare to the vistas I see as I turn off the expressway and know that in just a few minutes, I'll be home.

Sometimes when I'm coming home I will be extremely tired and feel as though I've had the weight of the world resting on my shoulders. I may even be feeling down in the doldrums and defeated, but something comes over me when I turn the corner and look at that house sitting at the end of the cul-de-sac. I'm home. When I get out of that car and push the door closed behind me, walk down the walkway and open the door, all of those feelings of defeat and exhaustion just don't seem to weigh me down the way they did a few minutes before. I guess the reason is that home offers me love, security, comfort and peace. I'm surrounded by those who love me the most . . . I'm home. There's nothing quite like the feeling of sitting down with your family at the "supper table," holding hands and praying as a family, and then laughing and eating, and just going over the events of the day. I'm home.

The words of B.J. Thomas, when he strums the chords to "Home Where I Belong" certainly communicate the desire of my heart. Home is just where I belong. There's no place like it, no place that can compete against it. No matter where I am, I get lonesome and homesick for my home in the suburban area of Atlanta, Georgia. But, you know, there's another home that's been provided for us. The Bible says, *"I go to prepare a place for you"* (John 14), and that, too, will be home. One day, because of our faith in Jesus Christ, we'll all go home.

† † †

HOW GOD MEETS OUR NEEDS

Sam Carrol was a student at the University of Oregon when a public appeal was made to help him procure a typewriter. Carrol, a 39 year old man, had no control of his arm and leg movements, and the only recognizable sounds he could make were "yes" and "no."

However, at the University's Speech and Hearing Center, he learned to type words on a typewriter with the assistance of a stick strapped to his head. Thus, the need for a typewriter of his own.

There was a tremendous response to Sam Carrol's need. Immediately, an 80 year old woman without family or friends, sent a donation of twenty dollars. Also, an ex-convict who, at one time, had been temporarily paralyzed, sent a contribution with a note attached which read: "I know what it is like to be paralyzed."

These and other people were happy to respond to Carrol's need. But, they were only able to respond because they knew about his need. Carrol had a legitimate need which he was not ashamed to let others know about. As a result, his need was met.

There are those about us just as unlikely as the 80 year old woman and the ex-convict who would be able and willing to help us meet a need in our lives. When we have a need, whether it is physical, emotional, or spiritual, we shouldn't be embarrassed or afraid to let someone know about it.

God will often answer our needs through other people, and He may not always work through the people we expect! And, remember that when God uses another person to meet our needs, His blessing will be two-fold: He will bless the person with a need by meeting that need, and He will also bless the one who was willing to be His instrument.

† † †

LET THE FEELINGS YOU PASS TO YOUR CHILDREN BE POSITIVE

I once heard a story of a young bride who was fixing one of the first dinners she and her husband shared together. For this very special dinner the bride decided to bake a ham. In preparing the meal, she cut off both ends of the ham before putting it in the dish. When her husband asked her why she fixed the ham that way, she replied that her mother had done it that way. At a later date when they were having baked ham at her mother's home, the young husband casually asked his bride's mother why she cut off both ends of the ham. The mother just shrugged and said that she really didn't know, but her mother had always done it that way. Finally, the young man asked the grandmother why she cut off both ends of the ham before she baked it. The grandmother eyed him suspiciously, and then stated, "because my baking dish is too small."

The way these women prepared their ham dinner had been passed from grandmother to mother, and then on to the granddaughter, and all because of a baking dish that was "too small." In much the same way we pass down to our children, and if we aren't careful, to our children's children, certain fears or behavioral patterns. One of these is rejection. The fear of rejection begins early in childhood as the child encounters its first "no." The child soon becomes a toddler, where he hears "no" more often. Then moving into adolescence, as teenagers seek to establish their own independence, the words "no" and "you can't" are often viewed as rejection of themselves as persons.

The circle must be broken at some point. If this feeling of rejection has been passed down to you, don't be content to pass it on to your children. You can learn to see yourself in a different light. You can begin to see yourself in light of how God sees you. God looks at you and sees someone that He loves. He sees you as someone who is so valuable to Him that He sent His Son to die just for you. You are someone who is so valuable to Him that all of the resources He created were made available to you. We must learn the truth of God's love for us -- and accept ourselves as being valuable. The Bible commands us to *"love thy neighbor as thyself . . ."* Too often people read that and realize that they are to love their neighbor without seeing that they are commanded to love themselves in order to love their neighbor. When we love ourselves, the feelings we pass on to our children and our grandchildren are feelings of love and self-worth instead of rejection. Don't keep cutting off the ends of the ham just because Mama did it. You might find that it was simply that her baking dish was "too small."

3
The Way of Motivation

IN THIS CHAPTER . . . .

I Want To Get Involved!
With The Help Of God, You Can!
What Do You Want To Live For?
Life Is Too Short To Be Little
Personal Example Is The Best Motivation
The Best Investment You Can Make
Don't Stand And Let The World Pass You By
Plan To Win
Using The Long Strokes Of Life
A Man Of Stone

I WANT TO GET INVOLVED!

Oliver Clarke of Pulaski, Va., was presented the "Good Samaritan Award" of the American Police Hall of Fame. Oliver received this award for heroism in saving the life of a three-month-old child who was trapped in a wrecked automobile.

Because of receiving the award, Oliver's good deed was publicized, and very soon cards and letters began to pour in from people that she did not know. She was not prepared for the number of letters that arrived praising her for her heroism. Ms. Clarke could only respond, "I did not realize how much kindness there is left in people."

Why did Ms. Clarke stop and help while other motorists continued going -- who just passed on by? This same question could be asked of the Good Samaritan that Jesus speaks of in the Bible. Why did he stop when others passed by?

The answer, I believe, is that they chose to get involved in the lives of people. While most people have the tendency to continue going on down the road and fail to get involved, the Good Samaritan made a different choice.

And so must we. If we are to show the love and concern for others that Jesus brought to us, we must be the one to make the different choice -- we must "get involved." After all, this is what Jesus taught in the parable of the Good Samaritan. It's what Jesus meant when He said, *"Go and do thou likewise"* (Luke 10:37).

† † †

WITH THE HELP OF GOD, YOU CAN!

How often when we have been requested to render service to the community or through the ministry of our church we've simply said, "I can't." We allow ourselves to believe that we really can't. In light of that we need to be reminded that:

-- Einstein could not speak until he was four years old, and did not read until he was seven.

-- Beethoven's music teacher said about him, "as a composer he is hopeless."

-- When Thomas Edison was a young boy, his teacher said that he was so stupid that he could never learn anything.

-- F.W. Woolworth was 21 when he got a job in a store, but he was never allowed to service customers because, "he didn't have enough sense."

-- Walt Disney was once fired by a newspaper editor because he was thought to have "no good ideas."

-- Author Louisa May Alcott was told that she was incapable of writing anything that had or would ever have any popular appeal.

Perhaps some have been informed so long that they can't, that when they are requested to do something worthwhile or constructive, they really believe that they can't do it.

An individual whose life has been characterized by negative, defeatist attitudes will have the following two results: (1) failure resulting in unhappiness and disappointment and (2) demonstration made to the world that Christ has not made a difference in the life of that individual.

The world will never be drawn to, or seek to emulate, a life that does not radiate confidence and joy that grows out of a genuine faith in the Lord.

We need to adopt the motto of the apostle Paul when he said, *"I can do all things through Christ which strengtheneth me"* (Philippians 4:13).

WHAT DO YOU WANT TO LIVE FOR?

Just suppose (and I pray it never happens) you are walking down a street and someone ducks out of a dark alley, puts a gun in your ribs and says, "I'm going to kill you." You then begin to plead, "Here's my money and my watch. Take anything you want, but please don't take my life! I want to live!" The gunman pauses for a moment, then says to you, "What do you want to live for?" Now, what do you say to a question like that?

Another similar situation could take place in a doctor's office. Suppose you are informed that you are critically ill with only a short time to live. You desire for the doctor to do anything he possibly can to spare your life. You say to him, "Doctor, you've got to help me! I want to live!" Then the doctor matter-of-factly replies, "For what do you want to live?"

I know of a college philosophy professor who begins each new term by announcing to his class, "I want you to write one paragraph, less than an entire page, on your philosophy on life." Now, suppose you are in his class? What would you write? What is your philosophy on life?

The answer to the above question stresses the truth that life must have a goal to give it direction. Life must have a purpose in order to give it motivation. Life must have an over-riding priority to help us make decisions day by day. Otherwise, life is empty and meaningless. And unfortunately, empty lives are common. Billy Graham recently asked a college president, "What is the number one problem on college campuses today?" The President summed it up in one word -- "emptiness."

The tragedy of this day and age is that many of us have so much to live with and so little to live for. Jesus spoke to this issue of life when He said, *"I have come that you might have life, and that you might have it more abundantly."* Abundant life is life with real purpose and meaning. It is not just a result of prosperous careers or close relationships with family and friends. But, our emptiness can be filled with the purpose and meaning that comes through Christ!

LIFE IS TOO SHORT TO BE LITTLE

The great philosopher Disraeli stated that, "Life is too short to be little." In just seven words, this philosopher expressed a thought that could change your life.

The brevity of life is expressed in Scripture like this, "*. . . For what is your life? It is even a vapor, that appeareth for a little time, and then vanisheth away*" (James 4:14). My understanding of a vapor goes back to my days as a young boy. My mother cooked on a big gas stove then, and when I would come home from school, there would often be a big pot of beans cooking. They would have been simmering and bubbling all day long. When I walked into the house, the first thing I would smell was the delicious aroma of those beans. I'd rush over to the pot and lift the lid, and as I did, just for a second, you could see the vapor escaping from the pot.

Now, the Bible says that life is like that. So brief! When a person begins to understand this, it will lead him to think about the quality of his life. The attitude with which you approach this "brief" time known as life will determine the quality of your life. An attitude that says that because life is so brief, then I'm going to do everything I can to keep it from being little as well, will be the attitude of a winner.

The Director of Admissions at a large university made a statement that exemplifies the truth of that. He said that less than 50 out of every 100 students who enroll in a university ever graduate. He explained that this was not due to insufficient intelligence, or to finances, but was the result of their attitude. He added that they leave school because they do not like the professors, the subjects they are taking, or their fellow students.

Instead of letting your attitude be shaped by the circumstances of your life, keep in mind that life is brief, and you need to squeeze everything out of it that the Lord will allow. By doing that you can shape your attitude with positive factors. This is the kind of attitude that will give you a philosophy of life that says: Life is too short, so I'll make it big!

PERSONAL EXAMPLE IS THE BEST MOTIVATION

Howard Cosell recalled a startling conversation with a mother who said, "I don't care if he (an anonymous athlete) is on drugs or not. If he can hit, run, and throw, I want him to be my children's hero." Now, to me, that is startling. But read on. In 1975, Frank Zarb, former Federal Energy Administration Head, flew chartered flights that burned 19,000 gallons of fuel to make speaking engagements in which he encouraged energy conservation. Senator William Proxmire estimated that half of those flights were in plush Air Force jets that burned as much fuel in one hour of flight as the average American driver would use driving an automobile for an entire year.

Most of us have heard the old story of the Preacher who said, "Don't do as I do, do as I say do!" I daresay that not many of us would want to sit and listen to this kind of preaching. But the examples listed above are of the same philosophy. There is another example. Parents will continually warn their children about the use of drugs and marijuana, but they themselves continue to use another drug, alcohol.

We must begin to put all of this "madness" behind us and recognize that if we are going to be able to motivate other people, our personal example is far more important than what we say. It has been expressed like this: What we are speaks louder than what we say. Personal example will speak loud, long and clear, whether it is what we are saying with our mouths or not. A good example is a costly process, and that makes it difficult for many of us. It costs our time, our energy, and even our money.

Talk is cheap. Christians will speak out loudly, lovingly, and longingly about their theology or their beliefs. However, translating the jargon into reality -- personal example -- requires people who will model their vision after what they believe God has called them personally to do. We must give ourselves to being living witnesses for Christ so that modern disciples will become aware of an exciting new possibility, that of motivation through example.

THE BEST INVESTMENT YOU CAN MAKE

What is the best investment you can make in this day of double-digit inflation? Is it stocks or bonds? Or, maybe real estate is the answer.

One thing is certain, before you make an investment, you should seek wise counsel. People want their investments to be secure, and yet give them profitable dividends.

One television commercial illustrates this truth by telling us that "when E.F. Hutton speaks, people listen." We listen because we want to make the best possible investment.

This being the case, why not consider investing in people -- God did! God's investment was costly in that it cost Him the life of His Son.

Investing in people will allow you to reap rich dividends. The reason for this is that people are important to God. Now, what is important to God ought to be important to us, and when He speaks, we ought to listen. He tells us by His example to invest in people, and His is the wisest counsel we could ever hope to obtain!

† † †

DON'T STAND AND LET THE WORLD PASS YOU BY

If you've ever read *Alice in Wonderland,* you might recall the rabbit saying to Alice, "You have to run as fast as you can just to stay where you are." It seems that the rabbit was not just speaking to Alice, but to all of us.

This jet-space-age is a hectic one. Sometimes it appears to be passing us by. You might relate to the man on the expressway who was observing the 55 mile per hour speed limit while everyone else passed him by. We just cannot stand still in life. It's like riding a bicycle -- as long as you're moving, you stay up, but just try to sit still on a bicycle!

The Bible encourages us to "... *lay aside every encumbrance and the sin which so easily entangles us, and let us run with endurance the race that is set before us*" (Hebrews 12:1). When Paul stated that he was *"forgetting what lies behind and straining forward to what lies ahead"* (Philippians 3:12), he made it clear that he was still very much in the race of life.

We must be reminded that yesterdays are gone forever and tomorrow may never come. We have today and we must make use of it! We just can't afford to stand still while the world is passing us by.

† † †

PLAN TO WIN

To be a winner in life means that we will be driven by our desires. No consistent winner, regardless of who he is ever wins who didn't want to win. You and I will become what we think. If we think only negative thoughts, and of ourselves as failures, and as never winning, we will never win. Self Motivation is not something that is instilled in us at birth, nor is it something that is acquired by writing out a check. Motivation is something that is from within the individual rather than outside which excites that individual to action. It is the idea and the emotion that prompts us to be and to do.

You can be and do all that God desires for you to be and all that God desires for you to do. It is within you to do it if you will overcome your fear and simply replace your fear with the desire to achieve your goals. How easy it is to blame our failures on circumstances, God or Mom. It is far easier to sit back and blame rather than to stand up and do. The old cliche "it doesn't matter whether you win or lose, but how you play the game" belongs to a loser. You can determine that you will be motivated to be and do all that God desires for you to be and do.

The Bible summarizes it well -- *"I can do all things through Christ which strengtheneth me."* The sky's the limit! You can be! You can do! It will be dependent on you!

USING THE LONG STROKES OF LIFE

A young man, new on the job, was working diligently at his workbench one day fitting a piece of metal. He was working with vigorous, but very short strokes.

The boss came along and saw what he was doing and said, "Both ends of that file are paid for. Don't take those short strokes with the middle of the file, use both ends." With that the enthusiastic young worker started using both ends of the file, taking long strokes of the file. Soon he had the task completed.

I wonder sometimes in life if we do not often make the mistake of using the short strokes. It is common knowledge that we probably do not use more than a small percentage of the potential with which God has endowed us.

We limit our accomplishments by concentrating solely on the "short strokes of the file."

One is using the "long strokes of the file" when he is utilizing his time and talents to the very best of his ability.

Let's begin now to use both ends of the file! ". . . *Or whatever ye do, do all to the glory of God.*" (I Corinthians 10:31)

† † †

A MAN OF STONE

Stonewall Jackson is one of the three men who are hewn in stone on Georgia's Stone Mountain. Stonewall Jackson is a man who, in two years, moved his Army at a very rapid pace. So fast, that they became known as the "foot cavalry." This man was a very quiet, private person. He was a man of strong Christian character, who never smoked or drank. He was a man who was open to give God credit for every victory.

One might assume that these qualities existed in this man from birth. He was born like this -- but this is not the case. The truth of the matter is, that Jackson was a slow learner at West Point and he was remembered only for his strange stubborness at that institution. He consoled himself to the fact that he was going to be a Math instructor at Virginia Military Institute. This was changed with the coming of war. War brought about a change in this man's life and in his character. So much so that this strong, stubborn will made him known as a "man of stone".

You and I live in a day when it is so easy to be swayed from one band wagon to another. We have lost much of our "stubborn character". We've sold out to "situation ethics" and "humanism".

In an hour of crisis, Stonewall Jackson surfaced to be a man with a stone-like character. In this hour of moral crisis, it is time for us to surface to meet the moral crisis of this day and to stand for Christian character. In Matthew, Chapter Five, Jesus said, *"Ye are the Light of the World . . . Let your light so shine before men that they may see your good works, and glorify your Father which is in heaven."*

† † †

4
The Way of Commitment

IN THIS CHAPTER . . . .

Working For God Full-Time Or Part-Time?
Are You A Villain?
Caution: Detour In Life's Road
Does God Really Care? Yes!
Begin To Control Change In Your Life
Placing The Blame
Landing At The Wrong Field
Make Jesus Christ Your Standard
Thermometer Or Thermostat?
God Can See On The Inside
Cry Father

WORKING FOR GOD FULL-TIME OR PART TIME?

Before Ed's "Here's . . . Johnny" on the late-night TV, we heard "Here's . . . Jack." Jack Paar at that time was the M.C. of the Tonight Show. The format was the same then as it is today.

On one of Paar's "Tonight Show" broadcasts, he was discussing the remarkable work of Dr. Albert Schweitzer, who was a self-giving missionary doctor. This remarkable missionary, before the age of 30, had earned doctorate degrees in philosophy, theology, medicine and music.

Paar was recounting the accomplishments of this man who gave his life in a small, remote corner of Africa. Yes, Schweitzer was willing to give himself for his "little corner of the world" when he might have had the accolades of the world. After a long pause, Paar uttered these words: "You know, I would like to be a Schweitzer . . . if I could commute."

Paar was unaware that he was also expressing the opinion of many religious thinking people. So often we make this commitment: "Lord, I am willing to do great things for you . . . but only if I can do them when and how I want to."

We hold in reserve our own rights in doing God's will. We reserve the right for part-time rather than total commitment, and in so doing we never learn the meaning of the words, *"Come, take up your cross and follow me"* (Mark 10:21).

† † †

ARE YOU A VILLAIN?

Before you are so quick to answer a resounding NO, there are several things that we need to consider. We need to consider first of all that Jesus said that we are to be the salt of the earth. Now, we are being informed that salt is a villain. Books have been written to us with titles like, "Killer Salt," "Shake the Salt Habit," "Cooking Without a Grain of Salt," and "Halt! No Salt." These books are selling in the hundreds of thousands.

There is even talk of a new organization called "Saltaholic." The new emphasis on salt stems from some new medical information that informs us that the average adult consumes two to two and one-half teaspoons of salt a day. This is more than twenty times what the body really needs.

Nutritionists are now calling this diamond crystal the "number one food fear."

An estimated thirty-five million people suffer from hypertension and this expands to sixty million if mild cases are included. Nearly half of the population over sixty five years of age is affected. Dr. Lot Page, Chief of Medicine at the Newton-Wellesley Hospital, said, "The link between salt and hypertension is as firm as the link between high cholesterol and heart disease."

What we are hearing is that we are to "shake the salt habit."

In light of this, I hear the words where Jesus said we were to be salt. The kind of salt that Jesus is talking about, however, is not one where salt is a villain, but to be that which can cause people to be victorious over their circumstances. The kind of salt that Jesus is talking about is a salt which is a preservative. In the day in which these words were written, salt was used to prevent the decay of foods. Jesus said that we are to be that substance in a secular society which prevents "society rot."

In this respect, we are pictured in victory -- not as a villain. Let's really get salty.

† † †

CAUTION! DETOUR IN LIFE'S ROAD

One of the greatest fears in the mind of any preacher is the fear of not being where he is supposed to be at the appointed time. That fear finally caught up with me.

The time came when I was to preach at the church where I am pastor, and then travel to Covington to preach in a revival service on the same night. I had allowed enough time to travel to the church on time, but what I had not allowed for was a detour! I was one mile from the church when I saw the blue lights flashing. An 18-wheeler was in the ditch, and traffic was being diverted and the street was closed.

I followed directions onto another street, assuming that the detour would be a simple one and that I would soon be back on my scheduled route -- no problem! But suddenly I had one. When I made the turn to get back on the main road, it was a dead end. I went to several of the streets but was still unable to get back onto the road that leads to the church.

In the haze of confusion I had gotten lost and found myself going from one subdivision to the next. After a long period of time, I arrived back at the point of the accident, stating to the police officer that I must get to the church. His directions were complicated and time consuming. Once again I started out trying to follow his directions, and eventually arrived at the church thirty minutes late!

Having just held their longest service EVER, the congregation was patiently waiting. My explanation to them was, "I took the detour, but after I had taken it, I didn't know where to go."

Many people who travel life's road are constantly detouring off that which Jesus said is "straight and narrow" [*Matthew 7:14*]. But after the detour they are still left stunned, not knowing where they are going. The way of life is marked out clearly and there is not the apprehension and insecurity of not knowing which way to go.

"And thine ears shall hear a word behind thee, saying, This is the way, walk ye in it, when ye turn to the right hand, and when ye turn to the left."

DOES GOD REALLY CARE? YES!

A pastor and a barber were taking a walk through the city slums. Looking at the sad state of the surroundings, the barber said to the pastor, "This is why I can't believe in a God that you contend loves everybody. If your God were as kind as you say, how could He permit poverty and disease like this? He would not allow these poor people to be addicted to drugs and other character destroying habits. No, I cannot believe in a God that would allow such as this."

A period of silence was felt between the two when the wise pastor saw an approaching derelict. His hair was hanging far below his neck in a most unkempt manner. The stubble on his face indicated that he had not had a clean shave in days.

It was then that the pastor turned to the barber and broke the silence. You cannot be a good barber or you would not permit a man to continue to live in this neighborhood without a hair cut and a shave."

The barber responded instantly. "How can you blame me for this man's condition? I cannot help that he looks that way. He has never given me a chance to help him. If he would come to my barber shop I would cut his hair and give him a clean shave and make him look like a new man."

Again a period of silence, but shorter than the first. Then the pastor looked at the barber and asked, "How then can you blame God for these conditions? He constantly invites people to come to Him and experience His love. The reason people stay bound up in shackles of their own doings is because they refuse to take the invitation offered that "whosoever will may come."

A ray of light broke into the barber's understanding as he saw the point. God stands with open arms. His love is ready to be shared. However, for us to experience it and gain hope, we are individually responsible for making the step of acceptance of His love.

† † †

BEGIN TO CONTROL CHANGE IN YOUR LIFE

Living in a world of constant change, you need only to look around you to see things that are different from the way they were a short while ago. There was a time when I could go down to the barber shop and get a haircut for fifty cents. Now a coke costs fifty cents, and I don't go to a barber shop anymore; now it's a stylist shop. They don't give haircuts, either . . . they style your hair.

Another area where change is apparent is in the clothing we wear. Just when I have my closet stocked with wide ties, I look around and realize that they aren't in style. Now I need narrow ties. And it seems that the lapels on my coat are always needing either to come in a couple of inches or go out a couple of inches. People don't seem to buy clothes anymore because the old ones have worn out. We rush out to buy new things because that's what "they're wearing" now.

But it isn't just the clothes we wear or the way we have our hair cut that's changed. Our entire lifestyles have changed. One of the greatest influences in this change has been the television set. The A.C. Nielson Company, which is the major broadcast rating firm for the United States, has informed us that adults spend an average of over 24 hours a week watching television. For a child, the average jumps to thirty hours a week, and the "one-eyed babysitter" now occupies over four hours a day in the average preschool child's life. By the time a child reaches school age he has watched an estimated 20,000 commercials. When he graduates from high school, he will have spent fifty percent more time in front of the television than in the classroom.

Television has become our "window to the world," but a great part of that "world" is presented through the means of a 60-second commercial. Commercials are repeated over and over again, until the product being shown becomes important to us personally, though it may have meant nothing to us before, and would have continued to be unimportant had it not been presented so many times, in such an enticing manner. Because we see these commercials repeatedly, our lifestyle becomes geared to the things we "need" to buy. Many people are now "buying a new lifestyle."

It's time to turn off "the tube." This is a parental decision, and the parent must be willing to do the unthinkable and say to the family, "Tonight we aren't going to watch TV. We can talk, sit around, play games, or just read." After you've done this for a while, you might find that you've really gotten to know the person who has been sitting next to you, evening after evening, staring at the "one-eyed monster." And you might find that you are enjoying spending time with your children.

Change doesn't have to be haphazard, leaving you feeling as though you're on a runaway street car, able only to observe or "go with the flow." It's time that we control the change in our lives. Begin by taking control of what is being viewed on the television in your home, and you'll find that this has been a constructive, helpful change.

† † †

PLACING THE BLAME

Now it's Howdy Doody's fault. A recent TV Guide blamed Howdy Doody for the social unrest of the 60's. The article was quoted that "Howdy Doody represents one of the most authentically subversive TV shows in American history." The article said it portrayed the children as heroes and the adults as villains, bores, or the butt of jokes, spawning a generation's belief that they could never trust anyone over thirty." The article even went on to claim that Clarabel, the clown, was the first Yippee. This children's television show, that ran from 1947 to 1960, just seemingly underlines the fact that we've got to blame somebody. Even Howdy Doody.

We must remember that God has given to every one of us the freedom of choices, and I am the sum total of the choices that I choose to make. Maybe we need to begin again to sing the song, *"It's not my brother, it's not my sister, but it's me, Oh, Lord, standing in the need of prayer."* It's always somebody else's fault. It's high time that we stop blaming Howdy Doody and take a long look at ourselves.

LANDING AT THE WRONG FIELD

Lowell Ferguson was a Western Airlines pilot who had the misfortune of acquiring the nickname "Wrong Field Ferguson." Ferguson was also required by Western Airlines to take a refresher course on how to approach airports, and was demoted from his classification as captain.

Now, all of this came about as a result of a mistake that Lowell made. His mistake was that he landed at the wrong airfield. Lowell was instructed by field navigation aids to land at Sheridan, Wyoming, but rather than use the instruments on his jet, he chose to rely on his own experience and eyesight. Doing just that, he landed his plane at Buffalo Airfield, which was 35 miles away from his intended destination.

The Buffalo Airfield had not been designed for jet aircraft, so the runway on which Lowell landed was much smaller than runways usually required for a jet. Lowell managed to land his craft safely, though, and that made him a hero in the eyes of the people of Buffalo. They designated a day in his honor and even got up a petition requesting that Western Airlines not be too hard on Captain Ferguson. Their reasoning was that "anybody can make a mistake." Western Airlines did not see the incident in quite the same way as the people of Buffalo. To them it was a very serious matter, because Ferguson had deviated from established procedures.

God has established procedures for us through His Word. There are times when we are tempted to "fly" by sight or to "fly" by feelings rather than by faith. We choose to ignore the navigational aids of the Word of God. Invariably, though, when we trust our own feelings and our own sight, we'll miss the runway that God has prepared for us. It takes "landing in the wrong field" in life to make us stop and really look at what we've done . . . and go over the basics of obedience and trusting in the divine instruction given in His Word.

† † †

MAKE JESUS CHRIST YOUR STANDARD

One of the most often used excuses for not coming to church is the old "I'm As Good As" syndrome. Someone will begin to make excuses for their absence from Church or Sunday School, and the first thing they'll say is, "Well, so and so goes to church all the time, and I'm as good as he is . . ." Psychologically, what this person is doing is excusing his or her behavior by the actions of others. Now, this practice can cause problems. I read an interesting story that really illustrates what can happen.

It seems that during a bad wind storm, the arm of a TV antenna was blown off. Well, this particular antenna belonged to a TV repairman. The man knew that his antenna was broken, and every time he turned on his TV set he was reminded that it needed to be fixed, but he just never got around to it. There were so many other people who needed his services in repairing their TV's that he just didn't have time to fix his own.

Well, one day the repairman's next door neighbor decided to invest in a brand new outdoor TV antenna. After all, he reasoned, if the expert next door had a TV antenna on his roof, then he probably needed one, too. The man decided that he didn't need to hire someone to put the antenna up, all he had to do was make sure it was just like the TV repairman's! So he drilled the lead-in hole in the same spot on the roof, secured the base in the same manner, and then turned the antenna in the same direction. Finally he stepped back and studied his antenna. He looked from his antenna to his neighbors, and something was wrong! So he reached up and yanked an arm off of his brand new antenna. Now, it was just exactly like the expert's! The only problem was that he had imitated its faults as well as its virtues.

There is something to be learned from the bad experience with the TV antenna. When we use the old cliche', "I'm as good as . . .," we need to remember that we're just comparing ourselves to another person -- one who has faults as well as virtues. There is only one perfect standard, and His name is Jesus. The next time you're tempted to compare yourself to someone else by saying, "I'm as good as . . . ," keep in mind that just being as good as someone else may not be good enough. "So and so" is not your standard; Jesus Christ is.

THERMOMETER OR THERMOSTAT

In most homes, a thermometer and a thermostat can be found. Both of these objects provide a useful service. The purpose of a thermometer is to register, record, and reveal the temperature of its environment.

When the surrounding temperature rises, the thermometer will also rise. Likewise, when the surrounding temperature drops, the thermometer will also drop. Hence, the thermometer is controlled by its environment. In essence, it does nothing more than reveal its surroundings.

Now, what about a thermostat? It functions in exactly the same way. It also has the ability to record, register, and reveal the temperature of its surroundings. However, unlike the thermometer, the thermostat has one important characteristic that makes it totally different. The thermostat not only has the capacity of determining and revealing the temperature in your home, but to change it as well. Depending on its setting, the thermostat can activate either the air conditioner or the heater to make your home either cooler or warmer than it is outside.

All the world can be divided into two categories of people: thermometers and thermostats. Every person will fall into one of the two groups. Those who are "thermometers" are victims of their environment, controlled by their circumstances, rising and falling with them. They live their lives with the defeated feeling that nothing they can do will bring about change. Their lives simply reveal their surroundings.

Then, there are those who refuse to be manipulated by their environments or circumstances. They are "thermostats." They do not allow their surroundings to dictate what sort of person they should be. Rather than simply recording and reflecting the norm of the day, they set about to change undesirable circumstances.

This change is accomplished by the Inner Power living within. God supplies the power we need to live victoriously and triumphantly over outside pressures or problems. This power comes only from the abiding presence of the Lord.

"And do not be conformed to this world, but be transformed by the renewing of your mind, that you may prove what the will of God is, that which is good and acceptable and perfect" (Romans 12:2).

† † †

GOD CAN SEE ON THE INSIDE

The term "non-invasive" is used to describe the procedure now being used in the study of ancient Egyptian mummies. This method permits scientists to study mummies without unwrapping them or cutting into their remains. Modern X-rays and sonar devices produce pictures of the skeleton structure and the internal organs without any alterations in the mummy's condition or appearance. You might say that this technique is a good example of "really looking through a person!"

When dealing with people, the Holy Spirit does not practice the "non-invasive" method. Instead, Hebrews 4:12-13 tells us: *"The Word of God is living and active and sharper than any two-edged sword, and piercing as far as the division of soul and spirit, of both joints and marrow, and able to judge the thoughts and intentions of the heart. And there is no creature hidden from His sight, but all things are open and laid bare to the eyes of Him with whom we have to do."*

God removes the wraps that hide our souls and cuts into the very center of our beings. He knows us much better than we know ourselves, and He loves us more than we can imagine. The Bible says that when we draw near to God, God draws near to us. So let us draw near to Him, knowing that our souls are fully exposed in His sight, so that we may experience the joy of an open and vital relationship with Him.

† † †

CRY FATHER

It always disturbed me for my mom to tell me that Uncle Joe was coming to visit. I just did not like Uncle Joe. The reason is that the first thing he would do when he came in would be to catch me and hold me between his knees and tickle me under the chin until I cried out, "Uncle!"

In my mind's eye I can see him coming into the house even today, making a beeline for me, laughing the whole time, catching me between his legs and making me stay there until I cried out "Uncle."

On one occasion I preconceived in my mind that I just would not cry "Uncle." He could do all that he wanted to, but I'd never do it. I would just grit my teeth and bear it. However, after several minutes of this fun time for him -- and agony for me -- it was easier to simply cry "Uncle."

Well, I'm not a little boy any longer, and Uncle Joe has gone on to heaven. I've moved on into the adult world, yet there still seem to be the pressures of this life that close in around me and trap me. The things, and occasions, of this world, seem to want to keep me trapped until I cry out "Uncle."

Having learned the truth about the many traps of life, I personally have learned that when the world traps us, and seems to be forcing us to cry out "Uncle," the avenue of escape is not crying "Uncle," but learning to cry out to the Father! When we've learned to cry out to Him, knowing of His love for us, we find the escape hatch to the pressures of this world.

We can learn the meaning of these words, *"Our Father which art in heaven . . ."* Matthew 6:9.

† † †

5
The Way of Worship

IN THIS CHAPTER . . . .

He Found What He Was Looking For
Raiders Of The Lost Ark
Seven Deadly Words
We Respect The Bible, But Don't Read It
Witnessing For The Lord In His Own Way
It's The Little Things That Matter
The "Sleeping In Church" Syndrome
More Than Mortar
Is There A Church With No Problems?
Excuses

HE FOUND WHAT HE WAS LOOKING FOR

One man went to church on Sunday morning and he heard the organist miss a note in the prelude; he saw a teenager talking when everyone was supposed to be bowed in silent prayer and he felt like the usher was watching to see what he put into the offering plate. Boy, did that make him mad! He caught the preacher making a slip of the tongue in the sermon five times by actual count. As he slipped out through the side door during the closing hymn he muttered to himself "never again! What a bunch of clods and hypocrites!"

Another worshipper went to church on Sunday morning. He heard the organist play an arrangement of "A Mighty Fortress" and he thrilled to the majesty of it. He heard a young girl take a moment in the service to speak a simple moving message of the difference her faith makes in her life. He was glad to see that his church was sharing in a special offering for the hungry children of Nigeria. He especially appreciated the sermon on that Sunday. It answered a question that had been bothering him for a long time. He thought, as he walked out the door, "How can a man come here and not feel the presence of God?"

Both of these men went to the SAME church on the SAME Sunday morning and each found what he was looking for. When you go to worship Sunday morning, what will you be looking for?

† † †

RAIDERS OF THE LOST ARK

The motion picture hit "Raiders Of The Lost Ark" has drawn long lines at the movies. This film deals with a fictitious attempt by the allied and German forces to find the ancient Ark of the Covenant in the World War II era.

A great deal of interest in the Ark of the Covenant has been generated by this film. The movie-goer must realize, however, that the film is fictitious. The result of the interest is in what the Bible has to say about the Ark of the Covenant.

The creation of the Ark was commanded by God. The Ark was a chest of Acacia wood, about 47 inches long, 27 inches wide and about 27 inches high. The overlay of the Ark was pure gold. On the lid of the Ark was a Mercy Seat, fashioned between two cherubims.

Now, originally the Ark was made for the sole purpose of holding the two stone tablets on which the Ten Commandments were engraved. The Ark of the Covenant also contained Aaron's rod which budded and a golden jar of manna, (that which fell from heaven to feed the Hebrew children during the wilderness wandering).

The Ark was placed in the Holy of Holies room of the Tabernacle. It was here that the High Priest entered once a year to claim God's forgiveness by pouring the blood sacrificed on the Mercy Seat.

The Ark was not only a symbol of the presence of God, but it was symbolic of the power of God. As time passed the Israelites began to substitute the symbol for the reality. The power was thought to be in the material of the Ark rather than in God Himself. One thing we can learn today from the symbolism of the Ark of the Covenant is the lesson that the Ark should teach us. We must be extremely careful that nothing -- not a church, not a church building, not a preacher, not a denomination, not a form of worship, not even the Bible itself -- becomes a substitute for a personal, continuing relationship with God.

SEVEN DEADLY WORDS

I recently read a newspaper article that stated there were too many counties in most states. The writer pointed out that most county boundaries were established long before the first automobile was built. While small counties were necessary during the horse and buggy days, in our modern world of fast automobiles and good roads, such small boundaries are no longer useful. In fact, combining three or four counties into one larger county would cut down greatly on duplicated services. This would result in better service to the tax payers at a lower cost.

In order to prove his point, the writer of the article interviewed thirty people at random. The reaction of the people was not what he anticipated. While the writer thought that he had stumbled across a really great idea, he soon found that he was the only one who felt that way. Not one person of the thirty people interviewed thought the idea had any merit, even though it would provide them with better local government at less cost.

Now, the thing that this research really gives evidence of is what could be referred to as traditional thinking. The traditional thinker's mind is always paralyzed. He reasons like this, "If it's been this way for a hundred years, it must be good . . . so why change it?" If there is any one place where the traditional thinker is right at home, it's in the church. The seven most deadly words of the church are these, "We've always done it this way before."

With so many people thinking this way, we often find ourselves, within the framework of the church, locked into what I refer to as the "boat of tradition." We will never know the joy and the excitement of new ideas and new approaches in our worship and work for the Lord until we are, first of all, willing to get out of the "boat of tradition." Don't allow the seven deadly words to keep you from trying new ideas. Be willing to get out of the "boat." You'll find that the water's fine.

† † †

WE RESPECT THE BIBLE, BUT DON'T READ IT

The Bible is the most revered book in the country. However, it is also little read! It seems that most people have respect for the Bible, but few ever read it.

This is the conclusion of "Christianity Today" magazine, based on a poll it commissioned to the Gallup organization. Forty-five percent of the persons polled could not name more than four of the ten commandments. When asked what Jesus said to Nicodemus in one of the most famous passages in the Bible, only thirty percent of the protestants answered correctly with, *"You must be born again."*

This situation is illustrated by a humorous story I heard. The story is that on Sunday morning, a new pastor stopped a young boy on his way to Sunday School. Wishing to get to know the boy, the pastor asked him who tore down the walls of Jericho. The boy immediately answered, "I don't know who tore them down." Then he added defensively, "But I know that I didn't do it!"

The pastor was astonished at the boy's reply. He decided that he must talk to the boy's Sunday School teacher. Relating the incident to the boy's teacher, the pastor was shocked when the teacher replied that he knew the boy very well, and if the boy said he didn't do it, then he didn't do it!

Well, by this time the pastor was just beside himself. He called an urgent meeting of all the deacons and told them of the incident, including the teacher's reply. He concluded by asking them what should be done. It was then that one of the deacons said, "I make the motion that we not cause any trouble. Let's just fix the walls and forget this whole matter."

This humorous story illustrates the truth of Gallup's findings -- most people respect the Bible, but few read it.

† † †

WITNESSING FOR THE LORD IN HIS OWN WAY

He was not too well educated, and his manner was somewhat crude and rough. He became a Christian and was on fire for the Lord, and was constantly asking the pastor to help him be of some genuine service to his Saviour.

In desperation, the pastor handed him a list of ten names with this explanation: "These are all members of the church, but they seldom attend our services. Some of them are prominent men of the city. Contact them any way that you can and try to get them to be more faithful. Here is some church stationery you may use to write them letters. Get them back in church."

The man accepted the challenge with rugged determination and enthusiasm. About three weeks later, a letter from a prominent physician in the city reached the church office. His name had been on the list. Inside the letter was a check for $1,000 and this note:

"Dear Preacher: Enclosed is my check for $1,000 to make up for my missing offerings. I'm sorry for missing worship so much, but be assured that I will be present this coming Lord's Day and every Lord's Day following. I will not by choice miss services again. Sincerely yours, John Doe, M.D.

"P.S. Would you please tell your secretary that there is only one "T" in dirty and no "C" in skunk!"

† † †

IT'S THE LITTLE THINGS THAT MATTER

Not long ago, the United States government thought we were under a "red alert." Believing that we were faced with a Russian attack, they instantly sent bombers carrying nuclear weapons into the air. Three long minutes passed before it was discovered that a computer failure had caused the false alert. The cost of replacing the defective computer part was only 49 cents. Such a little thing was about to cause a nuclear holocaust!

In Ontario, a nuclear station also suffered the consequences of a false alert. A small screw came loose from a valve link, causing an entire warning system to be activated. The whole nuclear plant had to be shut down until the missing screw was located and replaced.

Just like the cases of the faulty computer part and the missing screw, the entire work of a church can be brought to a standstill as a result of what may appear to be only a little thing. Little divisions, little criticisms, little grievances -- these can paralyze the lives of a group of Christians.

Church history has proven that it will not be the onslaught of martyrdom or the oppression from without that will bring the ministry of the church to a standstill. It will always be the little things that bring the unity of the church to a halt. Let's try to avoid the little things that can cause big problems and focus our attention on the things which have heavenly value!

† † †

THE "SLEEPING IN CHURCH" SYNDROME

It happens quite often in church -- perhaps more often than we preachers would care to admit -- worshippers begin to nod and yawn, and it sometimes requires a quick pinch or punch by the person sitting next to them to bring the sleepy heads snapping back to attention. It's the old "sleeping in church syndrome" that many times proves to be quite embarrassing.

This sleeping dilemma not only affects worshippers in a church service, but even those in the presence of royalty. Several years ago when Fred Mulley was the British Secretary of Defense, he was seated beside the Queen and Prince Phillip. A photographer came by and snapped a picture of the Defense Secretary slumped in his chair, apparently dozing during the royal occasion. Later, in an apology to the Queen, Mulley referred to the incident as his "momentary lack of attention." He fervently apologized for sleeping in the presence of royalty.

Sometimes we forget that when we worship our Lord, we are also in the presence of royalty -- the presence of the King of kings and the Lord of lords. Being in His presence is certainly not the time for slumber! It is the time for the giving of our undivided attention. Not only is staying awake physically important, but it is equally important that we stay awake mentally. When we experience true worship, we will be richly blessed, for we will have been in the presence of royalty. Royalty in the highest sense of the word!

† † †

MORE THAN MORTAR

"USA Today" recently reported that "there's a boom year in church construction." Money spent in the USA's churches and related to buildings was up 25% in 1983, says the commerce department. This increase in building has been attributed to the increasing interest in religion, and this is causing church building to increase. Another statement said that the increase could be due to fast growing conservative denominations that place a premium on group activities, and thus need more space.

Spending hit 1.7 billion in 1981, then fell off to about 1.5 billion in 1982. But spending in October, the latest month available, hit a seasonal adjusted annual rate of 2.3 billion, which is up 43% from October of 1982. We're building bigger churches, but we must remember that churches are not built with brick and mortar. Jesus didn't come to die for bricks. Jesus came to die for people. People are the church.

Now, people need buildings and space, but let's be reminded that in this time when church building is booming, that the prime objective in building is to minister to people. It was people for whom Jesus died. People are the church, and Jesus said to Peter, *"and upon this will I build my church."* The church that Jesus built is one that's built on people.

† † †

IS THERE A CHURCH WITH NO PROBLEMS?

Have you ever thought about finding a Church where there were no problems? Well, you would probably spend your life looking. You would hop from one Church to another, constantly seeking, never satisfied. But you would still look, believing that somewhere you would find it -- the perfect Church -- the one that's just the way you want it. The problem is, for a Church to have no problems, it would have to have no people. So, the minute you move in, it ceases to be perfect.

There is a fictitious story of an airline executive who was so tired of the constant hassle he received from people that he felt he just couldn't take it any more. One day the aeronautic engineers of his airline created what was certain to be, for the executive, the perfect airplane. It was completely computer automated. There would be no crew to contend with. What a fabulous idea . . . no more errors, no more hurt feelings, no more problems!

The day for the first demonstration flight came and everyone was filled with excitement. Everything went splendidly. The plane taxied down the runway, took off, and climbed to its cruising altitude. As everyone settled back to enjoy the flight a voice came over the speaker.

"This is your computer pilot speaking. Welcome to the first completely computer automated flight. You may have lunch whenever you prefer. Push the button on the left side of your seat and it will be served automatically. I am in complete control of the aircraft. Sit back, relax, and enjoy the flight. I assure you, nothing can go wrong. Nothing can go wrong. Nothing can go wrong. Nothing can go wrong . . ."

Well, you can see the point to that story. What was true with the computer operated aircraft is true for our churches. They are never going to be perfect. As long as there are people, there are going to be areas to continue to improve, and people who continue to need encouragement and enlightenment. The words of an anonymous poem pretty well sum it up:

*"Some perfect Churches there may be,
But none of them are known to me;
Yet we work and pray and plan
To make our Church the best we can.*

† † †

EXCUSES

"Well, it's raining today and we'll just not go."

"You know, our company is going to be here this morning, so we'll just not go to church today."

"I really don't feel up to it this morning."

"You know, that preacher has a way of getting 'longwinded.'"

"The Falcons will be kicking off about 1:00 p.m. We'll miss the opening kickoff if we go to church, so we'll not go today."

You've heard these "reasons" and more, or you may have used them yourself. I could not help but think of some of these reasons as I recently read an article about the church in China. Some of the news that is now coming out of China telling us of the things that took place during the cultural revolution has been frightening. There was a suppression of Christians that took place during that "cultural revolution." Religion was fiercely attacked! Christians from "house churches" suffered harsh abuse. An example of that abuse happened in the Chinese town of Xiaan, when Christians were forced to kneel before a pile of burning Bibles. A former "Bible woman" was beaten to death inside a church in Beijing. Some of the faithful Christians in that church were forced to watch. As they watched this frightening scene, they were instructed to recant or suffer the same consequences. The "Gang of 4" brought continual suppression of believers during that terrible age.

And yet, in light of that, the church in China continued to flourish. While it is impossible to obtain precise statistical data on the progress of the church there. Some research was done recently by the "China Church Research Center". Their findings have provided reliable information about this "church growth explosion". The Research Center estimated that there are between 25 and 50 million believers meeting in house churches in China.

One example of this is the Henan Province which has 111 counties. Of these 111 counties, 15 of them have an average of 100,000 believers each. One county had only 4,000 believers in 1948, but now those 4,000 believers have grown to over 160,000 believers. There are a thousand meeting points scattered over 20 communes in this province.

I have difficulty trying to imagine a Chinese Christian, having come through this terrible persecution, having the same excuses as some listed above for not worshipping. Can you imagine them waking up on a Sunday morning saying, of all things, "It's raining, I'll not go to worship today"!

† † †

6
The Way of Difficulty

IN THIS CHAPTER . . . .

Grief Must Be Expressed
Stones Of Adversity
      . . . Or Stepping Stones To Success?
Safety, Security And Satisfaction
Turning Failure Into Success
What Does Tomorrow Hold?
Follow The Navigator
Always Have A Thankful Heart
Enjoying Change
And You Think You Have Trouble
The Eternal Safety Hatch

GRIEF MUST BE EXPRESSED

Some time ago I was traveling in north Georgia. I travel frequently, and invariably when I pass a church, it attracts my attention. I always study them, wondering who the pastor is, and how they are doing. Well, on this particular afternoon I went by a little country church, and as I passed I noticed an elderly woman standing alone in the cemetery. I drove on down the road about a mile, but I couldn't get that elderly woman out of my mind. Finally, I stopped the car, then turned around and drove back.

I knew that I would frighten her by getting out of my car and walking toward her, so I just stopped the car and called through the window. I told her that I was a Baptist preacher looking for such and such a church, and asked if she could tell me where it was. With that, she began to give me directions. When she finished, I asked if it would be all right if I got out of my car for a minute. She said that it would, so I walked over to stand with her. As I approached, I saw that her cheeks were wet with tears, and I asked, "Ma'am, who is that that's been buried there?" You could tell that it was a fairly new grave.

She looked at me and said, "Well, that's my husband. I lost him a few weeks ago. I come out every afternoon and visit for a few minutes. Then I'll be all right, and I'll head on back home." Before I left, I asked if we could pray together, and we bowed our heads and thanked God for life after death.

I've thought a lot about that elderly woman expressing her grief. It reminded me of a story in one of Pearl Buck's books entitled, "The Mother." In the story a young man is leading his mother to the cemetery. They are mourning the loss of her youngest son. She tells the elder son to "go away and leave me for a while, and let me weep." When the elder son hesitates, she insists passionately, "leave me, for if I do not weep, then I must die."

Grief must be expressed. It must be experienced if a broken heart is to be mended. Give people permission to grieve, for grief is a God given remedy to help heal broken hearts. That's why two of the most powerful words in all of the Word of God are these: *"Jesus wept."*

STONES OF ADVERSITY...
OR STEPPING STONES TO SUCCESS?

Many years ago a young man inherited from his father a very large tract of land. Because of the unusual number of rocks in the area, no one had ever tried to farm the land, and it had become overgrown with vines, bushes and trees. The young man's father had known his son well, and realized that if the son was to make a success of farming the land, he would have to be challenged to do so; he would have to have a goal to work toward. And so, the bequest had a condition attached to it. The son would have to live on the land for five years. If within that time he succeeded in making a living from the property, it would remain his, but if he failed to meet the conditions of the will, the property would be given to someone else.

Determined to succeed, the young man went to work. First he cleared a small area of the land and built his house. As he cleared the land, he made piles of the rocks that were pulled from the earth. He used the best rocks to build his fireplace and chimney, and then he walled his garden with them, and laid his walks. Tons of the remaining rocks were sold to his neighbors for similar purposes. When all of the rocks had been cleared away, he tilled the land and began farming. Soon he was one of the most prosperous men in the neighborhood.

The moral of this story is simply that the things we view as "stones of adversity," the very things we think are holding us back, often become the stepping stones of accomplishment. I'm sure you sometimes feel like "things have gotten a little rocky lately." Well, the next time you find yourself feeling that way, try to look at the "stones" you're encountering as challenges, because they just may be the tools that God is using to make your life into what He intended it should be. *"The steps of a good man are established by the Lord..."* (Ps. 37:23). He knows just how "rocky" your path has become, and He will be a *"light unto your path"* (Psalm 119:105). He'll show you the way to overcome the "rocks."

† † †

SAFETY, SECURITY AND SATISFACTION

He was only 18 years old. He was a long, long way from home in a country that he had never seen before, with people that he had never been around before. He was out on "recon" patrol. It was dusky dark with the sun just beginning to set. It had been a clear day and the sun was beautiful as it began to sink behind the trees. It was the kind of day that one would think would be a great day to be home, sitting on the porch, just having eaten supper. It was the kind of an evening that would make your mind begin to wander and your thoughts to go back to home.

The daydreaming stopped abruptly and suddenly for the enemy began to open fire. The group of seven dove suddenly to the ground as the enemy continued to bombard them. It was the young man's job to stand and return the fire, to spray the area so that the other six men could advance. As he rose to cover the area with machine gun fire, he felt a stabbing sharp pain in his right shoulder. In the blinking of an eye a second shot hit him in the right arm and then a third, piercing into his leg and knocking him to the ground.

On the ground an 18 year old boy from Virginia lay on the edge of a forest south of DaNang in Vietnam. It's a long way from the back porch of a Virginia home.

As he lay there with the sun setting, gripped in fear, he looked just above the tree line and there was a cross rising just above the trees. He could see nothing else but the cross. He lay there all night. The only thing he could remember as the sun went down and darkness fell was the cross just above the treeline.

The next day this group of Marines made their way through the trees to an opening and there stood a little church that was riddled with bullet holes and bombed out, almost totally destroyed. The only thing standing was the steeple and on top of the steeple, the cross. It was the same cross that a scared, 18 year old Marine saw as the sun went down. The impression that cross made on him as he lay there all night was a sense of comfort in the midst of his confusion and fear.

As I listen to the story that was shared with me, it brought to mind a reality. In the life of a Christian, while all around us can be confusion, chaos and fear, the one source of comfort that everyone can turn to is the cross. It will always stand up high enough to be just "above the tree line" to show you the way to safety and to security and to satisfaction.

† † †

TURNING FAILURE INTO SUCCESS

There was a man who experienced a number of failures in his life. In the year 1831, he became a failure in the business world. In 1832 he was defeated for the State Legislature. He tried again in business in 1833 and failed there also.

In 1836, he suffered a complete nervous breakdown. In 1838, he suffered defeat for the Speaker of the House. In 1840, he was rejected as an Elector in the Presidential election.

In 1843, he ran for a seat in the United States Congress, but once again was defeated. However, this man just refused to be a quitter. He refused to stop trying.

In the year 1860, this same man was elected President of the United States. This man was Abraham Lincoln, perhaps one of the greatest Presidents of all time.

We suffer defeats in our lives, but our defeats can only defeat us when we allow ourselves to be totally defeated. The Bible says, *"I can do all things through Christ which strengtheneth me."*

That's right! I can do all things through Christ. The inward strength to deal with my problems comes from an inward power. This inward power enables me to succeed over my failure.

"God sponsors no losers." You are a winner. Recognize that you are a winner. Having recognized this, now enter into a "Winner's Attitude." And who knows? The sky can be the limit for you, too.

† † †

WHAT DOES TOMORROW HOLD?

I'm sure you've heard the old cliche', "another day, another dollar". What would happen if you changed the words slightly to read, "another day, another . . ." -- what? What will another day bring? What will happen to us tomorrow? In today's world there is much to worry about. Anything could happen at any moment which could forever change the course of our lives.

There are those eternal pessimists who can't enjoy today for fear of what tomorrow might bring. They live on the two little words, "What if." What if they become ill; what if they lose their job? What if nothing goes the way they feel it should? Then there are those who are always asking, "Why me?" Without realizing it, they are keeping themselves in a perpetual state of discouragement and defeat. This "what if" and "why me" pessimistic outlook keeps them struggling and robs them of the joy of living today.

In Greek mythology, it was the cruel king of Corinth, Sisyphus, who was condemned to spend eternity rolling a stone up a hill in Hades. He would get the stone to the top of the hill only to have it roll back down to the bottom where he would begin the process over and over again. For all eternity all he would ever know would be the struggles of pushing that stone to the top. The pessimist mentioned above spends the day pushing the stone to the top of the hill.

What unspeakable peace and glorious joy comes from knowing that there is a purpose for all manner of tragedy, small or large, that befalls us. Let us remember that we do not know what tomorrow holds, but we do know Who "holds" tomorrow, and the One who "holds" tomorrow is the same One who will be holding us today, for no man can pluck us out of His hand. John 11:28.

† † †

FOLLOW THE NAVIGATOR

A terrible tragedy occurred when the freighter, Summit Venture, crashed into the Sunshine Skyway Bridge over Tampa Bay. A large section of the bridge collapsed and hurled 31 motorists and bus passengers to their deaths.

The investigation of this horrible incident revealed that John Lerro, who was piloting the ship when it hit the bridge, had been involved in seven prior incidents during his three and one-half years of service. However, because the previous accidents were not serious, the board simply dismissed them.

We Christians are also on a voyage. We are traveling from earth to Heaven. Some people refer to this voyage as our pilgrimage. We have an infallible guide, a Heavenly Pilot -- the Holy Spirit, who will lead and direct us as we sojourn. If we listen to His instructions, we will never suffer a shipwreck, for He never makes a mistake or a miscalculation. Following His divine guidance will prevent us from crashing into "life's bridges."

† † †

ALWAYS HAVE A THANKFUL HEART

Deliverance from death often triggers an attitude of thanksgiving. This is illustrated by the following three news stories:

Last May, a French adventurer was rescued from the freezing Atlantic after his racing boat capsized about 1,000 nautical miles from the shore. "I thought of dying," he said, "but I didn't give up. I knew I'd freeze if I did. I'm very thankful, very thankful . . ."

Two university students found themselves still alive "thanks to the driver of the bus that plunged off the Sunshine Skyway bridge into Tampa Bay." The two students were on that bus, but changed to another when the driver told them they could save an hour by taking an inland route. "As far as I'm concerned, we had our guardian angels with us," said one of the students.

A Calgary woman "thanks God" for allowing her, her two daughters, and one of their friends to survive the "horror story" created by the erupting of Mount St. Helen's in Washington. On May 18, they were on their way to transport some horses back to Alberta. But, on their way, due to the poor visibility created by the ash from the volcano, their truck, pulling a trailer with four horses in it, ran over the side of a highway and down a seven-metre embankment. Amazingly, no one was injured, and the horses also survived.

The above three stories are filled with excitement. A capsized boat, a fallen bridge, an erupting volcano certainly capture our attention. Now, I've never been in any of these situations, but that's not the point. The point is that regardless of where I am as a child of God, He promises to *"never leave me or forsake me."*

† † †

ENJOYING CHANGE

I had only a small stack of wood left from last winter. All summer I would pass by the continually curing, finally split, hickory timber as I was mowing the back yard. Dreams of bitter cold evenings with a crackling fire, hot cider and my favorite football team on the tube would accompany my thoughts as I would labor during the steaming days of July and August. Well, fall came and went and my football team came and went and the warm days stayed along with a few pieces of my ready-to-burn firewood. Finally, I could take it no longer. Despite the 73 degree readings on the thermometer. I built a fire during the New Year's weekend. With all the family home it seemed an appropriate time for my cherished prized hickory, which burned with great speed and heat. Although we had to open the windows and turn on the ceiling fan, it was a beautiful fire. Of course, the weather has now decided to behave as it should this time of the year and has left me without longing for cold nights; however, there is no crackling fire, as I am left with a bare spot in the back yard where the fire wood should be, having spent my energies and my fuel at an inappropriate moment.

Well, the seasons and the weather seem to remain virtually the same for long periods of time, only to one day change abruptly. However, in actuality, week by week, minute factors moved the environment from that most extreme condition on the one end of the thermometer to the most extreme, uncomfortable state at the other end. These small changes mean little to us in the dead of winter. Our bodies just insist that we will be cold forever. In the day to day endeavors of work and family it is so easy to view our current situation as a submitted way of life with few variations on the horizon. We feel that if we could avoid any great calamity or tragedy then life will just go on as it should; a day by day, moment by moment life of doldrums.

There is the dread of change, for change can bring out our insecurities. Just as the weather experiences a change, our lives will experience change. We will go through different changes in life, just as we go from one season to the next, from hot spring to cool fall to the dread of a cold winter to the balminess of spring. There is constant change taking place. It is important how we adjust to the change, realizing that our security must not be in the circumstances, but our security must rest in our faith in the Lord, for He never changes. He is the same yesterday, today and forever.

I've learned to enjoy the changes of the seasons. That's why I love living in the deep south, for we can experience the seasonal changes. In life, we will experience the seasonal changes and they too can be enjoyable, if we'll learn that the Changeless One controls our changing lives.

† † †

AND YOU THINK YOU HAVE TROUBLE

In DesMoines, Iowa a stockbroker by the name of Gary Lewellyn realized his dream of becoming "filthy rich." His life-style exemplified his success in his business as a stockbroker. However, all of his success and all of his good fortune seemed to have come to an abrupt halt.

On March 31st Lewellyn withdrew one half million dollars in $100 bills from the Continental Illinois National Bank and Trust Company of Chicago and then vanished from sight. His car, parked at the airport, had two books left in the front seat. One book was "Catch Me If You Can," and the other was a Bible.

Lewellyn had reportedly misappropriated $2.8 million in Government Securities, and since then his troubles have been accumulating. A small army of government agents have filed suit against him, charging him with stock manipulations; the FBI has accused him of embezzlement; the Federal Deposit Insurance Corporation wants $9 million from him; the IRS says he owes the Government $3.2 million in taxes; and the Securities Investor Corporation is looking to him to be reimbursed for money lost from their customers. In addition to all of this, Deanna, his wife, has charged her husband with desertion.

Old friends and associates were stunned by all of the charges and reports that he left behind brokerage debts totaling $22 million. The delimma that Lewellyn finds himself in is one of his own making.

Reading the account like the one above makes one realize that maybe our problems are not as big as they seem. What happens, however, is that we let our nagging problems, that begin as something quite small, mushroom into a mountain and the end result is an emotionally draining experience.

I have no idea of how Lewellyn can be rescued from such financial devastation, but I do know how we can find relief from our day by day problems and troubles. A verse of scripture in the 10th chapter of Matthew, summarizes the solution when it says that our Lord is aware of the number of hairs on our head. He is certainly aware of all of our situations and He stands ready to deliver us from our heavy burdens when we reach the point of realizing that He can carry them much better than we ever could.

† † †

THE ETERNAL SAFETY HATCH

The other day I boarded an airplane in Miami, expecting to have a nice, restful flight to Atlanta. The plane took off, and after a few minutes the stewardesses went to work getting ready for dinner. The seat belt sign went off, and everyone started to relax and get comfortable.

About that time the Captain asked the stewardesses not to begin serving. Everyone had to return to their seats and buckle their seat belts. The Captain said we were going to encounter some turbulent weather. He was so right! A few minutes later we encountered a terrible storm. For what seemed to be a long time, the plane rocked and plunged to and fro, as we battled the turbulence. The flight was not a pleasant one.

Although I did not enjoy the experience on the plane, there was a feeling of familiarity about it. Many times in our lives, just when we are getting relaxed and comfortable, we encounter turbulence. Suddenly we are tossed about, running into obstacles at every turn. The smooth course we had been following has become a very rough, rocky path. And there is nothing we can do but sit and wait, with our seat belts buckled.

This experience is not unique to the people of our day. After Noah had finished building the ark, and loaded it with all the animals as the Lord commanded, he and his family encountered their worst storm. Without a doubt, they were tossed around inside the ark, probably falling or being knocked down many times. But the Lord did something very special for Noah. When he and his family were safely, securely inside the ark, "... *the Lord closed it*" (Genesis 7:16). The Lord closed the ark so that Noah could not fall out. To be sure, he fell down inside of the ark, but not out. At times, with the clouds hiding the sun, and the rain pouring, it had to look pretty dark, but the Lord was there, keeping everyone safely inside the ark.

The Lord does the same thing for each of us who know Him. We will stumble, we'll fall down, and sometimes things may look so dark that you can't seem to find the path -- or see the obstacles that block the way. But we cannot fall out. The Lord brought us into His love, His grace, the assurance of His salvation, and when we were safely inside, He closed the door behind us. We can never fall out!

7
The Way of Celebration

IN THIS CHAPTER . . . .

Count Your Blessings!
I'll Be Home For Christmas
Joy To The World, The Lord Hath Come
Doll Fight In Cabbage Patch
Christmas -- A Time To Enjoy With Your Family
Happy New Year!
Face The New Year With Certainty
The Meaning Of Christmas
Life Has Reality Through Jesus Christ
Make Each Day A Day Of Thanksgiving

COUNT YOUR BLESSINGS!

Thanksgiving Day! The children will be coming home. The turkey has already been bought and is in the process of thawing. The dressing will be mixed and the pumpkin pie will be made. Thanksgiving Day is here!

It is a day filled with overfilling from the table. It is a day of just sitting back and watching the football game. It is a day when we begin to think about the Christmas list because tomorrow the Christmas shopping spree begins. All of this is Thanksgiving Day.

Do you remember singing a song during this time called, "Count Your Blessings, Name Them One By One"? Why not try to do that? Why not try to count your many blessings. Just try to begin, just try to name them one by one! As you begin, you can name off the top of your head what would be the obvious . . . family, country, plenty of food, homes to live in. You'll begin to find out that the list is endless. You can't begin to name your blessings one by one because there's not time enough during this 24 hour period of time known as Thanksgiving to do that.

Why not try to summarize the blessings of God in a prayer this Thanksgiving Day? As you sit down with your family and any close friends who might be there and hold hands around the table, just thank God for the great privileges that we have as human beings of living in this land that is so filled with this bounty. The blessings of the Lord on this Thanksgiving Day cannot be numbered one by one. We just gather together, Lord, to thank you for your bountiful blessings. Happy Thanksgiving!

† † †

I'LL BE HOME FOR CHRISTMAS

One of my favorite Christmas songs is "I'll Be Home For Christmas." Every time I hear that song, my mind takes me back to my home at Christmas time. I can smell the turkey cooking, the cakes, cookies and pies baking, the fresh bread coming out of the oven; mulled cider and freshly grated coconut for the coconut cake. These are the memories of Christmases past and there "is no place like home for the holidays." Home at Christmas meant a gathering together of the whole family. Once again we would meet around the table to ask God's blessing and to thank Him for the bountiful year He had provided. It didn't matter if "things" were scarce because the love and fellowship of our family never was.

Those days are gone now; but only to the extent that I don't go home for the holidays anymore. Now home is here, and this is where the children come home for the holidays! Now I am not going; I am waiting. Months may have passed without seeing precious faces so very, very dear to me. Soon, soon, they will be here for Christmas. The excitement and anticipation is just the same as it was when I was a child.

Life has a way of changing things, though. In the changes of time there is, however, the changelessness of the warmth and love that was instilled in me when I was home for the holidays. At my home we pass on from generation to generation that warmth, acceptance and love. That which I received at home for the holidays will now be given to those I will be receiving for the holidays.

Without a doubt, this is the heart of Christmas. In reality, this grows out of understanding of what Christmas is all about. I have moved from, "I'll be home for Christmas" to waiting until "they come home for Christmas!"

† † †

JOY TO THE WORLD
THE LORD HATH COME

Well, it's here. It's the busiest time of the year for most people -- it's Christmas! The merchants are delighted over the economic forecast that the cash registers will ring up one of their best years ever during this Christmas season. The shopping malls are filled with shoppers, and the forecasters have indicated that people are buying "expensive" gifts this year.

Now for me, it's difficult to get a lot of "Christmas joy" in a shopping mall. I've found that, for some reason, I can go out and jog a couple of miles -- play tennis all afternoon -- walk around the golf course -- walk a mile and a half after parking my car just to get to the stadium for the ball game -- But after walking around a shopping mall for 15 minutes my back begins to hurt. It's far easier for me to find a comfortable place to sit and try to wait very patiently while my wife does the shopping.

As I sat waiting the other day I began to notice how everyone around me seemed to be in such a hurry, rushing from counter to counter, all with their shopping bags tucked under their arms. I watched as some of the parents got really provoked with their children, and one mama whipped her child there in the department store. I found myself getting very depressed and asking the question, "Is that what it's really all about?"

We see the answer to that question when we begin to understand that "Joy to the World" does not mean running over the shopping malls, spending our money and making the cash registers ring. What it does mean is that joy has come. He was born of a virgin, and His name is Jesus. He is what it's all about.

When you find yourself engrossed in the shopping and flurry of other activities that have become part of our Christmas celebration, stop to remember the real reason we celebrate is heard in the song, "Joy to the world, the Lord has come."

† † †

DOLL FIGHT IN CABBAGE PATCH!

Doll fight in Cabbage Patch? That's right. The race is on! All over the United States people are scrambling around, pushing and shoving, in an effort to get a "Cabbage Patch" doll.

This is the time of year to be joyful, but one woman in Wilkes Barre, Pennsylvania, probably isn't feeling too joyful right now. She suffered a broken leg going after a Cabbage Patch doll. Four other people were injured in that department store. In one store, a store official armed himself with a baseball bat to defend himself against the onslaught of people coming after Cabbage Patch dolls. The store manager of yet another store said, "My life is in danger."

As the sun came up over a shopping mall in Washington, D.C., crowds of anxious Christmas shoppers were already standing in line -- and had been for hours -- in the hope that they might be one of the fortunate people who got a Cabbage Patch doll. At another shopping mall in Anaheim, California, people stood outside locked department store doors screaming, "let me in, let me in!" The store manager said that they were crying, pushing and shoving each other in an effort to be the first one in the store.

Just when I think nothing else will surprise me, something always does. I am amazed at the things that motivate people. We can become so obsessed with getting a Cabbage Patch doll that we completely forget about the reality of life around us. As we enter most of the shopping centers, we pass by people patiently ringing a bell, collecting money in a black pot, so that they might be able to give food and clothing to the needy. But we hustle on by, shoving and pushing to get a Cabbage Patch doll.

"Tis the season to be jolly" -- unless you've been in a fight over a Cabbage Patch doll. "Joy to the World" -- except for those who are busy fighting over a Cabbage Patch doll. It really is a great time of year -- a joyous time of celebration and worship. It's sad to see that so many people have forgotten the real meaning of Christmas.

† † †

CHRISTMAS -- A TIME TO ENJOY WITH YOUR FAMILY

"I'll be home for Christmas, you can count on me." That's a line from one of the all-time favorite Christmas songs that people all over our country are singing now. And it's a desire shared by most of those people. All during the weeks before Christmas you'll find airport terminals bustling with people and train stations overcrowded as people watch for their trains. The highways across American will become crowded the week before Christmas as people in their cars or on buses all head for that special place . . . home. There's just no place like home at Christmas.

When I was younger, I would call my dad before Christmas and ask him what he really wanted for Christmas. I always knew the answer before he spoke it because it was the same each year, and I'd laugh as he told me, "Well, don't go to any trouble for me. All I really want is for you and the family to be home for Christmas." Sometimes I'd tease him and say that's just what he would get -- I was coming home, and just to surprise him -- there wouldn't be any presents! You know that I never did that.

Well, my children are grown now, and I have grandchildren. I've come to realize that dad wouldn't have been surprised at all if there hadn't been any presents for him under the tree, if we were all home for Christmas. Each year the wisdom in Dad's words grows a little clearer for me . . . it's my children's presence that I desire . . . not their presents. By and large, all of the presents under the tree -- although they're put there with a lot of thought and love -- are things we could do without. But having your family with you, your children and grandchildren, is something that cannot be replaced. This is the time of year for families to be together.

Christmas is the time we celebrate the birth of Jesus Christ, and that gives it special meaning for most of us. It's a celebration of the day that love and joy came into the world, through the person of Jesus Christ. I'd like to wish each of you a very happy and holy Christmas, and pray you will join with me in giving thanks that joy has come to the world, for the Lord has come.

HAPPY NEW YEAR!

Goodbye 1984! Hello, 1985! I don't know what you hold for me, 1985, but as I reflect back over 1984, I want to learn what 1984 has taught me so that when I start afresh with you, '85, I will be able to learn from my past mistakes.

If I could relive 1984, I would do some things differently. In some areas I would rearrange my priorities. However, 1985 offers to me a great opportunity to learn from my past so that I can help to design or direct my future. At the beginning of a new year is a good time to do that.

Now, not many of us can claim that we have not made some mistakes in 1984 which we'd like to remedy in the year to come. No mistakes of the past, no matter how great they were should at any time make any of us give up the hope and effort for a better tomorrow with fewer mistakes.

Consider the musician whether he or she be a violinist, harpist or pianist, a true musician if he misses a note would not throw the instrument away. He would simply finish the piece with the determination that when he plays it again he would not play the same mistake.

I heard the story of a famous artist that was asked the question, "Which has been your greatest work?"

The artist paused and thought a few moments before he stated, "The next one." That's the way I want to approach 1985. I see in it the challenge for my "next one." We must face the year with the hope and determination for a better tomorrow because of a better me.

There was an artist that reached the zenith of his fame and was heard lamenting, "It's too bad that I failed." His close friend thought for a moment and said, "Failure, you? You've achieved fame and fortune. What more could you ask? Why do you consider yourself a failure?" The artist then replied, "Because I've lost the hope of improvement." Now, if that were the case, then the artist is right. It is the person who has lost the hope of improvement that considers himself a failure.

Come on in, 1985, we're waiting. We've learned from 1984, we'll improve in 1985. We will approach 1985 with hope for a better tomorrow. 1985 holds for us the uncertainties of not knowing what the new year will hold for us. However, the one who holds 1985 holds us. Come on in, 1985, we wait with expectancy.

† † †

FACE THE NEW YEAR WITH CERTAINTY

As we begin the new year, it will bring forth a host of people who believe they can take current facts about our lives, and facts from the past, and then, with the use of various scientific methods, predict what our future will hold. We will be "bombarded" with the predictions of these people known as futurologists -- and indeed, the predictions have already begun.

Well, having watched over the new year predictions for over a decade, I've noticed that most of the futurologists have turned from humanistic optimism to bleak pessimism. One report given this year says we are running out of everything except people -- and to make matters worse, food prices are steadily rising because of the increasing demand for food and decreasing amount of available growing land. I could go on and on listing the predictions, but after a decade of reading them, I've found that the only thing I can depend on from these futurologists is that they hardly ever agree on anything. The reports vary from honest personal convictions to science fiction, from reports of increasing world hunger to Toffler's *Future Shock* and Orwell's *1984*. There is little agreement, and less certainty.

As we approach the new year, uneasiness about our future has for many, become a way of life. Some people are at their wits end trying to find a way to survive the "crisis of crises" that many of the futurologists are predicting. Others -- and especially among our youth -- are apparently trying to ignore the fact that there even is a future by escaping into a surrealistic lifestyle concerned only with drugs or alcohol.

We don't have to face the future in fear, running away from problems or worrying ourselves into a state of panic or even illness. There is an underlying principle -- a certainty -- that we can depend on. That principle is that our future, and so our security, rests in the hands of the One who created our world. The Psalmist described it like this, *"they cried unto the Lord in their trouble, and He delivered them from their distress; He made the storm be still, and the waves of the sea were hushed"* (Psalm 107:28-29).

We're faced with a great deal of trouble on our planet. With hunger in every country, civil unrest in most, and war in some, it doesn't take a futurologist to tell us that. But there is hope, and that hope is in the Lord. As we begin this new year, let's begin not as a pessimist, relying on man's abilities, but as a hopist, with our hope anchored in the truth and security of our Lord.

† † †

THE MEANING OF CHRISTMAS

I just love this time of the year, it is so very, very special. It is special for the whole family. We're not a family that waits just one or two weeks before Christmas before we begin to put up the decorations. As a matter of fact, our Thanksgiving afternoon is always spent in decorating our house. All the planning for the parties and activities are almost all together secured by Thanksgiving Day. We know that the family will be coming in. My wife is so cautious to select just that very special gift. I just love Christmas.

I love it because of the carols, although I can't sing. Someone has said that my singing is like a jailbird, "always behind bars and can't ever find the right key!" But my, how I love to try. How I enjoy singing *Silent Night* and *Joy to the World*.

I love the smells of Christmas. The apple cidar with cinnamon in it. The smell of pine. All of this tells me of Christmas.

There's a twinkle and a gaity in the lives of people. I love Christmas. People are laughing and acting as if they were children. It seems that families are a little closer at Christmas time. We are more concerned about the hungry people at Christmas time. We're bothered more about the man who has tattered clothes come Christmas time. We're always willing to drop money in the black kettle while the Salvation Army rings the bell because it's just part of Christmas time.

We view each day with anticipation. We begin to count the days until Christmas day. We just love being around children as we begin to see things through their eyes again. All because it's Christmas time.

We become even more religious at Christmas time. We think of the serene setting of a babe at Bethlehem. Sweet smelling straw. The beautiful animals. The wisemen and the shepherds, the angels singing their chorus. They remind us it's Christmas time.

How strange it is we've moved away from the real meaning of this time of the year for after Christmas day we're always in a hurry to get the decorations down. We race out to the malls to find what's on sale so we can exchange the things we really didn't like. That pair of pants that didn't fit, the suit we didn't like, and the list is endless. Then we conclude -- it's all over.

It need not be. Christmas ought to be every day. From the manger scene to the empty tomb, the Christ born in Bethlehem is so much more than a heartwarming holiday idea. The life that He gives is a year long reality. Christmas, the celebration of our Lord, is truly every day! Merry Christmas!

† † †

LIFE HAS REALITY THROUGH JESUS CHRIST

On December 8, 1980, John Lennon, the eccentric organizer of the Beatles whose music captivated audiences of every age, was shot and killed by a psychotic fan.

The Beatles came into being at a time of a great vacuum in this country. The Vietnam war was not accepted by a large portion of the population, including many people who participated in the war. It was the time of the assassination of our President and his brother, and of Martin Luther King. Student unrest, riots on college campuses, and bombings of buildings around the country were constantly in the news. The nation repudiated one President. The impeachment of a second was averted only by his resignation.

The Beatles became an idol to many. They expressed with their music the frustrations, the emptiness, the hollowness of life common to many people at that time. John Lennon was quoted as saying, "The unknown is what it is, and to be frightened of what it is, is what sends everybody scurrying around, chasing dreams, illusions, wars, peace, love, hate and all that. It is just an illusion. Accept that it is unknown, and it is plain sailing from then on."

In other words, what Lennon was saying was that life is an illusion. It is all unknown. There is no way to figure it out. There is no meaning to it. Why not you accept it? If you will, it will be plain sailing. Sailing into the unknown, the irrational, the inexplicable.

But for Lennon himself, life was not all plain sailing. As he walked from his home, a young man from Decatur, Georgia put an end to his life. Death came in the hard, harsh reality of a senseless murder. Lennon's widow called for prayer to be offered for his soul, and fans around the world gathered together for moments of silent prayer.

Life is not an illusion. Life is not simply sailing blindly into the unknown, not just chasing dreams. Deciding that there is no reality, accepting that there is no meaning or direction in life, only assures that you will miss the reality of your life. There is meaning to life. There is purpose, and there is direction. Two thousand years ago a baby was born in Bethlehem. The baby was the Christ child. His birth was the birth that was to bring "great joy to all men." Through Him we are offered life that has meaning, life that has purpose, and life that has direction. No, life is not an illusion, not simply sailing into the unknown. Life has meaning through the Christ Child, whose birth we celebrate at this time of the year.

† † †

MAKE EACH DAY A DAY OF THANKSGIVING

Thanksgiving Day! Thanksgiving Day is always a special day in my home. All of the children arrive home at the first of the week so we can share this time together. The turkey is put on to cook on Wednesday night, and early on Thursday my wife begins what will be for her one of the busiest days of the year. The favorite dishes of all of the family, which range from chicken and dumplings to french fries, will be prepared to be enjoyed by all.

The tradition which we enjoy so much today came about after a great deal of suffering and hardship. In 1623 a desperate band of Pilgrims launched their dreams and headed for a new life, in a new world. As they began their journey, no one realized how hostile their new environment would prove to be. During that long first winter they struggled with hunger and depression, disease, defeat and death. But they made it. Spring came, and then the summer, and finally it was time for the harvest. As the small group of people joined together to celebrate the bounty of their harvest, and to give thanks for their lives, they began the tradition of Thanksgiving Day which we still honor today.

When we look at the hardships that the Pilgrims endured, it's easy to see how they would be so grateful just to be alive, but sometimes we look at ourselves and our lives without that same feeling of gratitude. Giving thanks is easy to remember on Thanksgiving Day, but we should remember to give thanks every day. When John Wayne was dying of cancer, he was asked by an interviewer how he dealt with his approaching death. He replied that ". . . every morning when I wake up, I am so thankful that I've seen the light of another day. It makes me so happy that I can live another day." If a man facing imminent death can reach out to life in such a manner, should we respond to it with any less joy and thanksgiving?

It's good to gather together with your family and close friends to share in this special day, but let's not limit our giving of thanks to this day only. Each time the sun rises above the horizon, God has gifted us with another day. That day should be a Thanksgiving

Day. As you gather around the table this Thursday, make a commitment that you're going to seek to make every day a day of thanksgiving. *"O give thanks unto the Lord, for He is good: for His mercy endureth forever"* (Psalm 107).

† † †

8
The Way of Consolation

IN THIS CHAPTER . . . .

I'll Never Attend Another Football Game
Running The Race Of Life
Going From Winnersville To Losersville
Going For Gold
Winners And Losers -- And No Other Players
The "Big" Play
It Seems Everybody Loves A Winner
Football Mania
The Road Race And Life's Race
"Pac-Man" Is Representative Of Life

I'LL NEVER ATTEND ANOTHER FOOTBALL GAME

A pastor announced to his congregation that he would never attend another football game. The town being known as a "football town" began to press him for his reason to never attend another football game. "Well," he replied, "It's the same reason people never go to church. For instance, every time I go to the football game someone asks me for money at the gate. They even tell me how much to give. There were people all around me, but no one, I mean, no one, even spoke to me. And the seats, they were so hard. There was a fellow on the field known as the referee that ran things just the way he wanted them whether I agreed with them or not. Although I am a loyal fan, the coach never came to call on me nor to ask my opinion about the game plan. The band always plays the same tunes. I could hear better music anywhere. I noticed a lot of hypocrites around me. They were more interested in cokes and hot dogs than they were in the game. And I know for a fact that the only reason some of the ladies were there was to see what some of the other ladies were wearing. And, besides all that, I've bought a book on football and I can stay at home and read it and get more out of it than if I attended the game."

The town's people got the point!

† † †

RUNNING THE RACE OF LIFE

Stan Cottrell is a long distance runner from Tucker, Georgia. He is the man who recently ran across America. In 48 days, he ran from the city hall in New York City to the city hall in San Francisco, California. To accomplish this feat, he had to run a minimum of 70 miles each day.

Now, it goes without saying that Stan didn't just suddenly decide one afternoon that he was going to run across America, and just start running. Long distance runners just don't run like that! There must be both physical and mental conditioning before you even begin to undertake a long distance run, and especially if you set out from the city hall in New York City for the city hall in San Francisco.

The race of life is so much like the race of a marathon runner. However, many of us try to run the race of life without realizing that preparation is necessary. To be able to run the race of life, it is absolutely necessary to begin to build up our inner stamina. The conditioning that is necessary to run the race of life is not physical conditioning, but spiritual conditioning. It is the "inner man" which we must begin to build up.

Now, Stan Cottrell had to build up the outer man, his outer strength, to be able to physically withstand the journey from New York City to San Francisco. You and I must build up the inner man, our spiritual strength. To accomplish this, we must make sure that we are even running in the race. The starting gun sounds as we make a personal commitment to our Lord. To leave the starting block is one thing, but to continue to run is quite another. It will take "spiritual exercise" to run the race of life and run successfully.

† † †

GOING FROM WINNERSVILLE TO LOSERSVILLE

The Detroit Tigers were winners of the 1984 World Series. At the start of the season it became very apparent that this was the year of the Tigers. All year long they led their division, clenching their title and then moved on to the World Series to take care of the San Diego Padres in high fashion. Some sports columnists classified it as an overkill. The Tigers were winners.

It's amazing what winning a ball game can do to the minds of people. Outside of Tiger Stadium thousands had jammed together to begin the celebration. What was being celebrated was the winning of a baseball game and the winning of the World Series. As in most cases, what started out to be nothing more than a winning celebration abruptly turned into chaotic confusion. Before long somebody began to set off firecrackers; this led to a shouting match, pushing and shoving. When the police moved in, the unruly crowd began to curse and jeer at the policemen. Violence soon erupted.

The end result of winning the World Series was one person killed, a large number of people injured, several fires and the firebombing of a police car. All of this just for winning the World Series.

I find it a bit strange that such a reaction could come over a ball game. Yet we're not reacting at all to the number of abortions, to the number of people slaughtered on our highways by drunk drivers, to the reality that 44,000 people on this planet die every day from lack of food -- 34,000 of whom are children. Yet we go about our everyday activities and we're not the least bit concerned.

If this is what is meant by winning the World Series, maybe we're fortunate that Atlanta has never won. Winnersville can suddenly become Losersville.

† † †

GOING FOR GOLD

Late night television has caused me to go "blurry-eyed"! While I'm not generally a television fan, I've been fascinated by the 23rd Olympiad, which has been underway for the last two weeks in Los Angeles, California. Many people feared that the Russians' decision not to participate would prove detrimental to this year's games. As far as I can tell, it hasn't mattered at all.

The athletes on the U.S. team have been a credit to our nation. What a thrill it was to see our young people standing proudly as Old Glory was raised! There were no fists raised in defiance to our nation. As a matter of fact, many of the athletes wept openly while our national anthem was played. I must confess, I found that there was moisture in my eyes, too. It made me proud to be an American.

As in years past, California again became the site of a "gold rush" as our athletes swept the gold medals in Los Angeles. For the athletes, these few days have been the culmination of a lifetime of training. They didn't simply decide to be in the Olympics, and the next day walk out and compete in the event. Those who participated had given a lifetime of training for this event. In the interviews with the athletes, the thing that became apparent was the burning desire, discipline and determination that had been necessary to train their bodies, hour after hour, day after day. Each had one objective: to "go for gold."

Now I'm confident that I will never compete in the Olympics. I'll never have the experience of standing there while our flag is being raised, knowing that my commitment has paid off . . . that I've won the gold medal. But I am "going for gold." The Bible says that the streets of heaven are made of "pure gold." Through Christ I am part of the team, and I'm assured of a first place finish. I'm assured of winning the gold. *"I press toward the mark for the prize of the high calling of Christ Jesus,"* (Philippians 4:14).

† † †

WINNERS AND LOSERS -- AND NO OTHER PLAYERS

Well, we've waited for months -- with each game adding to our anticipation -- and it's finally here. That's right, it's Super Bowl 18! After months of excitement and frustration, joy and disappointment, this Sunday will mark the end of the 1983 football season. The Redskins and Raiders will compete in the final game of the season, and one of them will be declared the Super Bowl Champion. There will be winners and losers -- and no other players.

You know, our lives are a lot like that. There are winners and losers in life -- and no other players. You can't call "time out," you can't call in a substitute, and the game doesn't stop for injuries. You have to play, and you either win or lose. There are no other players.

Well, if you have to play, you ought to play to win. In I Corinthians 9:24 we're told, *"Do you not know that those who run in a race all run, but only one receives the prize? Run in such a way that you may win."* Every day of your life, in everything you do, you have the opportunity to win . . . or to lose. So why not win? The thing that will make the difference is a winning attitude, and that attitude is derived from a commitment to Jesus Christ. Jesus said, *"I came that they might have life, and might have it abundantly"* (John 10:10). He wants you to win!

Jesus gives your life meaning and purpose, and He enables us to live each day with all of the excitement and enthusiasm we'll see displayed in next Sunday's Super Bowl game. You are a winner through Jesus Christ. Live the abundant life! After all, if we have to play the game, and we know we're either going to win or lose, why not play to win? It's a lot more fun than losing.

† † †

THE "BIG" PLAY

The Miami Dolphins and the San Francisco 49'ers squared off Sunday, January 20th, for Super Bowl number 19. That which had its beginnings in the early spring of '83 came to a conclusion in the balmy weather of California. When Super Bowl Sunday finally arrived, all the sports writers had something to write about as they anticipated Super Bowl Sunday. While I was returning on a flight to Atlanta, I found myself in luck. Someone had left the sports section of the daily paper. Boy, was I fortunate! Quite normally, the reading material is *Woman's Day* or *Redbook* magazines. This was my day, for I found *USA Today's* sports page. As I settled back to enjoy my good fortune, I read an article on the great plays that took place in the different super bowls. I read of the great play in Super Bowl Five, where the Dallas Cowboys dove from the Baltimore two-yard line. Dwayne Thomas fumbled as he spun into the end zone and the Colts recovered and went on to win the game 16-13. I remembered Super Bowl 13, when in the fourth quarter Pittsburgh receiver Lynn Swann tripped over Dallas defender Benny Barnes on what quarter-back Terry Bradshaw called a "Hail Mary" side-line pass. The steelers went on to win it 35-31. Well, these were just a few of the great plays talked about in the past Super Bowls.

It had been estimated that there would have been one hundred and thirty snaps of the old pig skin, but only one truly big play. In a game like the Super Bowl, it takes the one big play that truly determines the winner.

In many ways life is like playing in a super bowl; however, in life every snap will count. It will not be just the one big play, for as we live day by day, every day is a big play day. Just to be able to live and enjoy the blessings of life makes every day playing like the "big play." That's why we have to live every day to the fullest while we remember that *"this is the day that the Lord hath made, we will rejoice and be glad in it."* Rejoice with me, won't you?

† † †

IT SEEMS EVERYBODY LOVES A WINNER

The Atlanta Braves were the most surprising team in baseball in 1982. Who would have ever believed that of all things, the Atlanta Braves would win their first 13 games of that season?

Now what is so important about that? Well, just this: until that year, the Braves just had not been winners. Since 1966, when the Milwaukee franchise moved to Atlanta, the Braves have been classified as one of the depressed areas of major league baseball. This recent streak has brought an end of "Losersville." This 13-game winning streak has set a new modern major league record for the most games won at the start of the season.

My, how attitudes toward the Braves have changed! More people met the Braves at the airport when they returned from a recent road trip visit than in earlier years sat in the ball park to watch them play. Cheers and shouts of people filling the stadium proves again that "people love winners."

As a Christian, quite often we exemplify attitudes and characteristics that show negativism and defeatism. And then, we can't understand why most people are "turned off" to our message. When these attitudes are evident, can you blame them?

The Gospel is the "Good News"! It is positive and highly motivational. There is no reason or need for us to stay in the doldrums of "Losersville." We are winners! The late Ethel Waters adequately summed it up when she said, "God don't sponsor no flops."

As we see from the events of the Braves, people do love winners. Let's begin to attract them to the Gospel with our "winning" attitudes.

† † †

FOOTBALL MANIA

Bring out the sweaters and jackets, it's finally here! The leaves are beginning to turn. The nights will get cool but the days will be comfortable; there is a crispness to the air that we don't feel at any other time of the year! I love the fall of the year. It's a special time. In conjunction with the wonders of nature there's another exciting addition to the fall of the year. Football mania has returned with Friday night high school games. The color and excitement of marching bands, screaming cheerleaders, and the high school gladiators as they take to the arena of combat make the pulse beat a little faster. On Saturday the lines are clearly drawn, whether it's spent in Grant Field or "between the hedges". These lines are seen whether we wear a yellow sweater or a red sweater. We display our colors and allow our feelings and commitments to be made known. Then comes the Sunday afternoon pro game. Finally there's Monday night NFL! It's a busy time of the year for football fever.

You cannot help but get excited when you find yourself in the stadium during the singing of our national anthem and then getting ready to watch the players kick off. The adrenalin begins to pump, the excitement is there. The emotions are expressed -- loudly! Football mania will bring it out.

I can't help but wonder why it is that we find it so easy to express our loyalties for our favorite team and yet find it so very, very difficult to express our loyalties to our Lord. One could draw the conclusion that we're proud of our team and somewhat embarrassed by our Lord. As we express our loyalties to our favorite teams, couldn't we be just as outspoken in our loyalties to our Lord? One final thought -- when you go to the stadium, you have to pay to get in, sit on hard, wooden seats, the people around you spill things on you, you're exposed to all kinds of weather and yet when it's over you walk out saying, "Boy, what a way to spend the day!" Yet, on a rainy Sunday morning, when it's time to go to church, how easy it is to say, "I might catch cold, we better not go today!"

Next time you go to the game, why not take a moment to make a small evaluation. Where are your loyalties greater, and is your object of devotion worthy of the same? Does a football game provide you with more excitement than a church service? Maybe it's time to change seats.

† † †

THE ROAD RACE AND LIFE'S RACE

July fourth in Atlanta, Georgia, is an exciting place to be. There are parades, fireworks at Stone Mountain, the concert in Chastain Park . . . the list of activities going on and on. One of the most exciting events is the annual Peachtree Road Race. Each year for the last 15 years, this race has attracted thousands of runners who come to Atlanta to race down Peachtree Street and then into Piedmont Park, a distance of 6.2 miles. The 1984 Peachtree Road Race included 25,000 runners, as well as thousands of spectators who lined the street to cheer the runners on.

Well, this year I made a commitment to run in the Peachtree Road Race. My reward would be the same as that of all who completed the 6.2 mile run . . . the 1984 Peachtree Road Race T-shirt. For weeks I conditioned myself for the race, extending my normal running distance to four, five, and then six point two miles. Early on July fourth -- extremely early -- I got up, put on my running shoes and headed toward Lenox Square. Thousands of people were already there, ready to run.

When eight o'clock came along, the crowd began moving down Peachtree Street, and I found myself moving right along with them. We climbed up "Cardiac Hill" (the hill at Piedmont Hospital), and then continued along, occasionally grabbing a cup of water or running underneath the spray. All the time I was telling myself that I was having the time of my life. I have to admit, too, that it was an exciting, fun experience, especially as I turned into the park and ran hard toward the finish line.

Having completed the race, I could not help but reflect on the comparison of that race to our lives. Every one of us is a competitor in the race of life. There are no spectators lining up to watch; we're all out there on Peachtree, and we're all running. There are times when we come to "Cardiac Hill" and really just want to stop, but there is no stopping in this race. We must run.

Within the life of the believer there is an inner strength, an inner resource, that enables that individual to run the race, and to run it successfully. He not only sees the gold at the finish line, but he has within himself the strength and motivation to keep running even in the midst of hardship and pain. He has that within himself because the Lord is faithful, and has promised to provide that strength. The believer also has the promise that there is a finish line, and when he crosses that line it won't be to receive a T-shirt, but to hear the words, *"Well done, thou good and faithful servant."* Run! Christian friend, run!

† † †

"PAC-MAN" IS REPRESENTATIVE OF LIFE

"Pac-Man" is an arcade game that has cost consumers an estimated $1 billion in quarters. It has been the hottest item in the video game market.

Pac-Man consists of little yellow, pie-shaped creatures that score points in the video game by gobbling up dots, colorful fruits and four ghosts that inhabit its world. Pac-Man, however, wilts and vanishes when one of the ghosts eats him. You will find the Pac-Man game in most grocery stores, in airports, and now it even goes into the home with a smaller version.

I went by the other day and dropped a quarter into the Pac-Man game. I saw my little man having to run either to gobble up creatures or get gobbled up himself. When I finished, having had my Pac-Man gobbled up, I continued on with my day realizing how much like Pac-Man we really are.

Most of our days are filled with the stress that comes either from "gobbling up" or "being gobbled up." Most people find themselves in the same boat, as daily stress chases and almost consumes them.

It is no wonder that heart attacks from stress, and other physical problems that stem from stress, are with us in record numbers. These physical problems should awaken us to the reality of what is happening. We refuse to listen because pausing for a moment, we think, might allow "the ghost" to gobble us up.

While moving so fast through life with the philosophy of "gobble up" or be "gobbled up" and living the life of Pac-Man, we fail to see the beauty of life all around us. We fail to see that which God has created in the smile of a little child, the beauty of dogwoods and the sweet smelling fragrance that comes from the flowers of the springtime.

Life is too precious. Life is too filled with dividends to live it at a Pac-Man pace. Let's hear the words of Jesus when He said, *"Come ye apart and rest a little while."*

And, sure enough, you'll not be gobbled up! But, you may be consumed with the beauty and the inner peace that comes from learning that life is worth living.

† † †

9
The Way of Society

IN THIS CHAPTER . . . .

It's Not As Bad As You Might Think
Americans Are Getting In Shape
War And Peace And The "Unthinkable"
We Live In The Midst Of So Much
      While Most Of The World Has So Little
Shadow Boxing
"Free At Last, Free At Last!"
Freedom Of Religion
"The Siberian Seven" Desire Freedom Of
      Worship
Our Treasure: Freedom Of Religion
Games Of Chance

IT'S NOT AS BAD AS YOU MIGHT THINK

Unemployment continuing its climb! The rate of inflation continues to eat away at our dollar. Because of this, many people are prone to think only the negative thoughts of our great country., Our nation is one of great affluency and prosperity. We live in the greatest society on Earth.

Let me illustrate our affluency. If we could compress the world's population into a town of one thousand people and keep proportions right, we Americans would number only 60. Yet, these 60 Americans would receive half the income of the entire town. The life expectancy would come to 70 years, while the other 940 persons would have less than 40 years life span. These 60 Americans would own fifteen times as much per person as all their other neighbors. They would eat 72% more than the maximum food requirements, while many of the 940 would go to bed hungry every night. Of 53 telephones in the town, Americans would have a total of 28. The lowest income group of the Americans would be by far above the average of the other townsmen. The 60 Americans and about 200 others representing Western Europe and a few classes in South Africa, South America, Australia, and Japan would be relatively well off. The other 75% would be poor!

We are tempted to think only the negative -- only the worst -- and to look at the dark clouds. We must realize the blessings of God upon our great nation. Let us just pause long enough to be thankful that we live in a land where we have been so richly blessed by God.

† † †

AMERICANS ARE GETTING IN SHAPE

We were, at one time, motivated to get in shape by Charles Atlas, who beckoned us on the back of our 10 cent comic books to "stop that bully from kicking sand in your face." Today we are motivated by much more than Charles Atlas on the back of a comic book. As a matter of fact, Americans are spending an enormous amount of money to just stay in shape. The cost for sport shoes alone last year reached $1 billion. Americans spent another $5 billion on health foods and vitamins, and you and I both know that any book on diet or exercise will sell. Last year the bill was $50 million for diet and exercise books.

Americans are also spending $1 billion on cosmetic surgery, $6 billion for diet drinks, $240 million for barbells and aerobic dance programs, $5 billion on sports togs and gear, $8 billion on gadgetry, from water filters and orthopedic shoe insteps to stop watches.

The body is "the temple of the Holy Spirit," says the Scripture; and we are commissioned of God to take care of our bodies, so I'm glad to see an emphasis on shaping up.

I'm also concerned, however, that we shape up spiritually. This will not be measured in cost of dollars, but in the cost of commitment. Just as it will take discipline to "stay in shape," to run when it's raining, to jog when we don't feel like it, to exercise when it's not convenient; it requires discipline to stay in shape physically.

My spiritual exercise would be measured in my discipline to spend time in the study of God's Word and to spend time in prayer. The cost for these two items will not be measured in dollars -- these two will never reach a $30 billion a year business, but rest assured they will cost. They will cost in time and they will cost in commitment. But the dividents are far reaching.

The body will be stronger by shaping up and the spirit will be stronger by shaping up spiritually.

† † †

WAR AND PEACE AND THE "UNTHINKABLE"

I read an interesting issue of *Time Magazine* entitled "Thinking the Unthinkable," which pointed out that we are now having to think about the unthinkable . . . the unthinkable possibility of an all-out nuclear confrontation with the Soviet Union.

Jonathan Schell's book, *The Fate of the Earth*, became a blockbuster before its official publication date. The book deals with the danger of nuclear war, and it is the result of five years of intensified interviews and study completed by Schell, on the various aspects of nuclear war.

Some of the responses to the editor concerning "thinking the unthinkable" contained words like: "The greatest social and environmental challenge in the history of mankind," "The U.S. and U.S.S.R. passed the point of over-kill several years ago," "In a nuclear war, nobody will be left out," "Reagan and Brezhnev should hold their first meeting in Hiroshima and Nagasaki. Those sites might help them in their deliberation." These are the words that are pressing us to the realism of the age in which we live.

At the end of World War I, Woodrow Wilson made a desperate try to end all wars. His valiant effort failed. On the cornerstone of the United Nations Building in New York City, these words appear: "*. . . and they shall beat their swords into plowshares, and their spears into pruning hooks; nation shall not lift up sword against nation, neither shall they learn war any more.*" (Isaiah 2:4)

Why can we put man on the moon and not put peace in a man's heart? Why is it that we can scatter satellites in space and yet not give to man the inner satisfaction of security? How is it that we can send the "Columbia" out into space and bring it safely home again, landing it in the precise point where it was intended; and yet we have not been able to land man in a sense of security on the planet earth?

There are so many unanswerable questions that all of mankind is asking. Is it perhaps that we are not asking the right questions? Can it be that man's real problems are spiritual problems and only when these are met can we know the peace that can come to the inward man?

WE LIVE IN THE MIDST OF SO MUCH WHILE MOST OF THE WORLD HAS SO LITTLE

As you sit down to a leisurely dinner this evening, perhaps you are not really aware of how much God has blessed you and your family. The major decisions you made about dinner were probably what kind of dressing to put on your salad, or whether to have ice cream or fruit for dessert. As you struggle with these decisions in this great land of ours, countless thousands of people around the world are also struggling with decisions about food. Their decisions are not the same as ours. They aren't concerned with whether to buy fruit or ice cream, or whether to use Blue Cheese or French dressing on their salad.

Every morning when you get up and begin to get dressed to go down to breakfast, trying to decide whether you want your eggs scrambled or over light, 40,000 people will awaken to die of hunger; 30,000 of them will be children. Each year 100,000 children become blind due to a lack of vitamin A in their diets.

In the past five years, more people have died of hunger than were killed in all the wars, revolutions and murders of the last century. It's a devastating awakening, isn't it? But read on. Every minute 28 human beings die of starvation. While we are getting anxious and irritated because we have to wait a couple of extra minutes in the fast food line to have our hamburger fixed just the way we want it, 56 people will die of starvation. They will literally die from hunger.

The United States spends 20 billion dollars per year on advertising. Just one tenth of that would save the world's children from protein deficiencies. And a word to our cat lovers. Two thirds of the world's catch of tuna comes to the United States; one third is used for cat food. Our garbage disposals probably eat better than do thirty percent of the people of this world. Ouch!

Oh Lord, forgive me when I complain because my eggs are scrambled too hard or my steak is too well done. I forget that I am so blessed, living in the midst of so much, while most of the world has so little. Forgive me, Lord.

SHADOW BOXING

When we have an enemy coming at us, we can usually define it; and we know how to stop the assault. Some have become so attuned in the Christian community to "defending the faith" that occasionally they find that they are actually "shadow boxing" and the foe is not even in the arena. Hardly a week passes that a person does not stop me and say, "Hey, Preacher, have you heard . . .?"

Rumors have spread in recent years that a petition to stop religious broadcasting has been filed by Madelyn Murray O'Hair. This is the woman who attempted to have prayer removed from the public schools. So, I guess Christians are a little jumpy when they think that she is working away at another freedom.

The irony of this situation is that the "shadow boxing" has been costly to the people who rose up to stop the rumored petition. $5.5 million have been spent in postage alone to voice opposition.

Roscoe E. Long, Chief of Policy and Rules Division of the Federal Communications Commission, speaking in Washington, D.C. recently declared, "There is no petition filed by Madelyn Murray O'Hair either old, new or pending or on its way." He further stressed, "There is not now nor has there ever been discussion about taking religion off the airwaves of the country."

The anti-O'Hair mail was averaging about 17,000 pieces per day at the FCC. It has now dwindled to about 6,500 pieces per day. We figured up that concerned citizens have spent more than $5.5 million in postage on a cause that never existed. It is a shame that these funds could not have been used for a worthwhile cause."

It is essential that we remain informed and we must be aware of things that would occupy our minds and preoccupy us. If we are not careful, we will find ourselves "shadow boxing" with ourselves while the enemy is able to move into another area unnoticed.

It is now time to let the community know that this fight is non-existent and those who support and listen to religious broadcasting can be thankful that this country of ours permits our freedom of religious expression.

While $5.5 million is a lot of money to waste, it does prove that many people are careful over their freedoms and it is encouraging to see that people took a stand when they thought it was needed. We must remain ready and be alert. In Ephesians 6:11 we are told, *"Put on the whole armour of God, that ye may be able to stand against the wiles of the devil."*

† † †

"FREE AT LAST, FREE AT LAST!"

I have never seen so many yellow ribbons! The joy all Americans feel as a result of the release of the 52 hostages prompted us to tie yellow ribbons not just on "old oak trees," but on anything and everything we possibly could! It was our way of proclaiming to the hostages, "Welcome home!"

During a week when we witnessed the inaugural ceremony of the 40th President of the United States, the overwhelming sentiment was not on Democratic or Republican issues, but on the return of the former hostages to American soil. And, on the Sunday of Super Bowl XV, the major emphasis was again on the former hostages being reunited with their families. Oakland Raider fans and Philadelphia Eagle fans joined together to celebrate the hostages' homecoming. The players, fans, and referees demonstrated their joy by wearing symbolic yellow ribbons.

In spite of the many diversities and dissensions that Americans face, we still are able to join together in unity when it comes to matters which affect the lives of our fellow countrymen. This is an encouraging note that there is still a strong bond that links us together as fellow Americans and enables us to put aside our differences.

The famous quote of Martin Luther King, Jr. need only be altered slightly to express the common heart of all Americans: "Free at last, free at last! Thank God Almighty, THEY'RE free at last!"

FREEDOM OF RELIGION

Today we, as Americans, enjoy freedom of religion. This freedom provides us with numerous opportunities for religious expression. For example, you can turn on the radio and hear Gospel preaching or Christian music. There is also Christian television that we can view. Yes, we are blessed in America with this precious freedom.

You may not be aware of what has happened as a result of this freedom. Did you know that:

There are 286,000 evangelical churches in the USA?

There is one ordained preacher for every ten church members?

There are 60 million evangelicals in the United States?

There are 60 thousand students enrolled in Bible colleges and seminaries?

There are 3,100 Christian bookstores in the United States?

There are 600 Christian radio stations in the United States?

There are many Christian television stations in the United States?

And yet the world lies in darkness! Who is going to tell the story? Who is going to come forth with the Gospel? Let it be us!

"To whom much is given, much is required." (Luke 14:48b)

† † †

"THE SIBERIAN SEVEN" DESIRE FREEDOM OF WORSHIP

I am sure by now that most of you have heard of the plight of the "Siberian Seven." You will recall that this group of seven Russian Pentecostals stormed into the U.S. Embassy in Moscow in June of 1978. Since that time they have been confined to small living quarters in the Embassy while trying desperately to emigrate to the United States to gain religious freedom. The Soviet Union has blocked every effort that they have made to leave the country and they refuse to return to their former lives in bondage. So, they wait . . .

World wide attention has been given recently to this small group of freedom-seeking Russians because of the hunger strike of two of their members.

Becoming aware of the trials of the "Siberian Seven" should bring everyone of us into a deeper and greater appreciation of our religious freedom. This is one area in the United States that we have taken for granted. On Sunday morning we can choose to go to church or not to -- but we have the choice. Not only can we choose to go but we can choose where to go. Most families will drive by several open churches as they go to the church of their choice. We do this, unconsciously aware of just how great a freedom we have.

Our religious freedom did not come cheap. Wars and bloodshed purchased this freedom. The price tag was high. We cannot allow the enjoyment of this freedom to be taken for granted.

I feel certain that if and when these freedom-seeking Russians are ever able to reach this country, a Sunday morning will never be taken for granted as they exercise the Freedom of Worship.

† † †

OUR TREASURE: FREEDOM OF RELIGION

Recently two men were arrested in Russia for bringing Christian literature into the country. Vasili Tashka and Ivan Oselsky were coming back from Romania when they picked up some Christian books, Sunday School lessons, and Christian tape recordings.

The border guard discovered this material and immediately arrested them. Soviet authorities accused the travelers of smuggling anti-Soviet literature into Russia and sentenced them to three-to-five year terms in a labor camp.

Now, just think about it! A crime to possess and distribute

Christian literature. In fact, it's a crime to read such literature in Russia.

It's very difficult for you and me, as Americans, to imagine such a system as that of the USSR. I wonder whether or not we Americans know how to appreciate the freedom that we have.

We have the freedom to distribute and disseminate our Christian faith freely in the United States. We can travel freely with no need of internal passports, and we can freely preach wherever we like in all of our 50 states.

Do we really treasure this freedom as we should?

† † †

GAMES OF CHANCE

In a quiet suburban neighborhood outside of Baltimore, Maryland stands the Nation's first State-supported Compulsive Gambling Counseling Center. The counseling center has been in operation less than one year, but already it has more clients than it can handle.

Officials at the center note that it usually takes from five to twenty years to develop into a confirmed gambler. To reverse the habit, they add, can require as much as two years for a full course of therapy and follow-up counseling.

We must be alert to the dangers that lurk in the shadows of gambling.

Legalized gambling now exists in 44 States. Nearly two-thirds of adult Americans now patronize casinos, bingo games, office pools, lotteries, horse and dog racing, off-track betting operations, and other legal gambling outlets.

The amount waged in 1979 in these different avenues of gambling was estimated to be $17 billion. According to a report of the Federal Commission on the review of national policy toward gambling, 80% of Americans approve of gambling in some form.

Estimates of the number of compulsive gamblers, however, have ballooned from around 4 million in 1976 to as many as 10 million today. It is apparent that we have got an ever-growing problem!

No one wants to become entangled in a webb of uncontrollable gambling. No one, I believe, sets out to become part of this national blight. But each gambler began somewhere.

We need to alert ourselves to the tendencies of "something for nothing" or "get rich quick" fantasies. As innocent as they are, I'm still prone to wonder if the cards we get when we buy a hamburger to take a chance to see if we've received a free one, when we buy a pizza and have a chance to see if we receive a free one or even to go 'double or nothing" open an unreal fantasy. As innocent as these are and as enjoyable as they are, do they serve as an open door for bigger games of chance? It's just a thought, but in light of the above statistics, it is note-worthy.

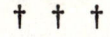

† † †